VISUAL QUICKSTART GUIDE

PHOTODELUXE
HOME EDITION 4

FOR WINDOWS

Jennifer Alspach
Ted Alspach

 Peachpit Press

Visual QuickStart Guide
PhotoDeluxe Home Edition 4 for Windows
Jennifer Alspach and Ted Alspach

Peachpit Press
1249 Eighth Street
Berkeley, CA 94710
(800) 283-9444
(510) 524-2178
(510) 524-2221

Find us on the World Wide Web at: www.peachpit.com

Peachpit Press is a division of Addison Wesley Longman

Editor: Nancy Davis
Production Coordinators: Lisa Brazieal, Amy Changar
Compositors: Rick Gordon, Debbie Roberti, Myrna Vladic
Cover Design: The Visual Group, Mimi Heft
Indexer: Rebecca Plunkett

ISBN: 0-201-35479-9

0 9 8 7 6 5 4 3 2 1

Printed and bound in the United States of America

✿ Printed on recycled paper

About the Authors

Jennifer Alspach is a nationally renowned artist and author whose artwork has appeared in a wide variety of publications. She is the author of several books and articles on computer graphics.

Ted Alspach is the author of more than 25 books on desktop publishing and graphics, as well as hundreds of articles on related topics. His books have been translated into more than a dozen different languages worldwide.

Jennifer and Ted are the owners of Bezier Inc., located somewhere in the middle of Arizona. They have five cats, a dog, a horse, a Gage, and a Dakota.

Special thanks to:

Nancy Davis, our wonderful, tireless, fearless editor at Peachpit, without whom we would have point blank refused to type a single word or edit a single image.

Special thanks to Steven Frank, whose motto of "a word a day, or else!" was often exceeded by two, sometimes even three times that amount. Steve's contribution to this edition has been enormous.

Mike and Robin Frank, for their work in creating and capturing many of the images that illustrate this book, and to Rachel and Jennifer for being so darn cute.

Scott Calamar at LightSpeed Publishing.

Amy Changar for getting things going on this book, and Lisa Brazieal for taking over and carrying things through to the end. The book looks great because of you.

And finally, everyone at Peachpit Press and beyond who helped move this book along until it hit paper.

TABLE OF CONTENTS

PART 2	**GUIDED ACTIVITIES**

| **PART 5** | **BUSINESS EDITION** |

PART 1

THE BASICS

The Basics

PhotoDeluxe is the easiest way to get started in image processing—the art of manipulating photographs in any number of ways. PhotoDeluxe provides all the tools you need to create some truly outstanding effects, as well as to correct existing images.

PhotoDeluxe caters to anyone who has ever been intimidated by powerful, complex software by providing something called "Guided Activities." These activities take you step by step through various procedures, explaining what to do and when to do it. (Guided activities are covered in depth in Chapters 4–6.)

Beyond the guided activities, there are many other things that you can do to your images, from jazzing up the color or adding special effects to replacing your Aunt Sophie's head with a jack-o'-lantern. (Advanced techniques are covered in Chapters 9–14).

But before you can learn how to do all that, there are some basics we need to cover, which is what these next few chapters are all about. Here you will learn what kind of computer you need to run PhotoDeluxe; how to install the software; what graphics terms such as pixels, resolution, and scanning mean; and how to get your photos or other images into PhotoDeluxe so that you can work with them.

1

GETTING STARTED

Getting started with PhotoDeluxe is a simple matter of installing the software (providing that your computer can run the software, which is something else we'll discuss), and getting in and out of the program. This simple chapter is a necessary first step before we can get to the really cool stuff.

What is PhotoDeluxe?

Simply put, PhotoDeluxe is a program that lets ordinary people do cool and useful things to photographs and other digital images. These "things" range from tasks as basic but indispensable as removing red-eye from photographs to more creative endeavors such as creating a calendar or greeting card that combines scanned photographs, clip art, and text.

PhotoDeluxe is brought to us by Adobe, the same folks responsible for very powerful professional graphics software such as Photoshop, Illustrator, and PageMaker. Photoshop is of particular interest to us, because it is the epitome of image retouching and enhancing software. Photoshop is so good that it quite literally has no competition. The only two drawbacks to Photoshop are its price tag (around $500) and its complexity. Neither of which are big drawbacks for people who make their living with it, but for the rest of us, Photoshop can be a bit overwhelming.

Which leads us happily to PhotoDeluxe, an image-editor "for the rest of us." PhotoDeluxe was created so that the average person could fix their photos or create attractive printed materials without having to invest big bucks or weeks of learning to do it. Most of your needs can be met by simply following along step-by-step with any of the dozens of Guided Activities. Once you've mastered those, you can switch to PhotoDeluxe's Advanced mode and explore and experiment to your heart's delight.

That said, it is also worth mentioning what PhotoDeluxe cannot do. PhotoDeluxe can't animate images, create a Web site, or create precise drawings or logos. If you want to do any of those things, you will need to get more software (and another book).

System Requirements

Before installing PhotoDeluxe on your computer you'll need to make sure your computer can run the software. We've listed here both the minimum system requirements (according to Adobe), and our own recommendations for a more robust system that will run PhotoDeluxe faster and more easily.

Minimum System Requirements

◆ 233 MHz Pentium II or 100%-compatible processor

◆ Windows 95/98 (or later) or Windows NT 4.0 with service pack 5

◆ 32 megabytes of RAM for Windows 95/98; 64 MB of RAM for Windows NT

◆ 100 MB of available hard disk space

◆ A color monitor and video card capable of displaying thousands of colors

◆ CD-ROM drive

Recommended System

◆ 400 MHz Pentium II or better

◆ Windows 95/98 (or later) or Windows NT 4.0 with service pack 5

◆ 64 megabytes of RAM for Windows 95/98; 128 MB of RAM for Windows NT

◆ 500+ MB of available hard disk space

◆ A color monitor and video card capable of displaying thousands or millions of colors

◆ CD-ROM drive

◆ Scanner with a SCSI or USB interface

◆ Digital camera (optional, but cool to have)

SYSTEM REQUIREMENTS

Installation

The first thing you'll need to do before using PhotoDeluxe is (obviously) to install it. Installation for PhotoDeluxe, like most Adobe products, is a simple matter of running the installation program included on the PhotoDeluxe CD and following the on-screen prompts.

To install Adobe PhotoDeluxe:

1. Insert the PhotoDeluxe CD in the CD-ROM drive.

    If Windows is set to auto-run CD-ROMs (which it almost always is), you will be presented with a brief animation (**Figure 1.1**) and a list of installation choices.

    If Windows is *not* set to auto-run CD-ROMs, you will need to double-click the My Computer icon, then the CD-ROM drive icon, and then the Setup.exe icon to start the installation process. Skip to step 3.

2. Click the Install button at the opening screen (**Figure 1.2**).

3. Read the Welcome information and click the Next button.

4. If you are in a country other than the United States, select your country from the list if prompted, then click the Next button.

5. Read the End User License Agreement and then click the Yes button.

6. At the installation Setup Type screen (**Figure 1.3**) click the Next button to accept the default installation type of Typical.

    If you want to pick and choose which parts of PhotoDeluxe are installed, select the Custom option before clicking the Next button. However, we highly recommend going with a typical installation the first

Figure 1.1 The CD Autoplay start-up sequence.

Figure 1.2 This screen starts the whole installation process.

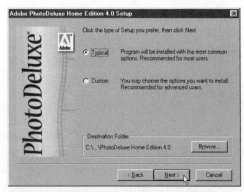

Figure 1.3 We recommend the Typical installation option.

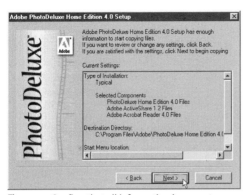

Figure 1.4 Confirm that all information is correct before continuing.

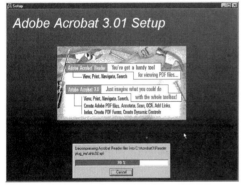

Figure 1.5 Adobe Acrobat is installed along with PhotoDeluxe and lets you view and print PDF documents.

time you install PhotoDeluxe to ensure that all necessary components get installed.

7. Enter your personal information and serial number (located on the PhotoDeluxe CD-ROM case) at the User Information screen and click the Next button.

You can register yourself as either a business or an individual. If you aren't sure which one you are, take this simple test: How do you answer your phone? If you say "Hello," then you're an individual. If you say something like, "Welcome to Northern Fiduciary Chemical Incorporated," then you're probably a business.

8. At the confirmation dialog box, click the Yes button.

9. At the Start Copying Files screen (**Figure 1.4**), review the information to make sure it is correct, then click the Next button to continue or the Back button to make changes.

The Setup program will install all of the components needed by PhotoDeluxe.

After PhotoDeluxe is installed, you'll be prompted to install Acrobat Reader 3.01 (if it is not already on your computer).

10. Click the Next button to launch the Acrobat Reader installer.

11. Click Yes to agree to the End User License Agreement (again).

12. Click the Next button to start the Acrobat Reader installation process (**Figure 1.5**).

13. Click the Finish button.

If you did not deselect the View Acrobat Read Me option before clicking the Finish button, you will need to close this file after reading it.

(continues on next page)

INSTALLATION

14. Click OK to exit the Acrobat installer.

After installing Acrobat, you will be presented with the first screen of a mercifully short ATM (Adobe Type Manager) installation.

15. Click the Finish button to end the installation process.

If the "PhotoDeluxe Home Edition online registration" option is selected when you click the Finish button, you will be prompted through a series of screens designed to gather marketing and research information about you and your software needs. The registration process allows you to register online or print a registration form which you can either mail or fax in to Adobe.

16. At the Restart Windows screen, click the OK button to restart your computer.

What is Acrobat?

In addition to PhotoDeluxe, the installation process also installs Adobe Acrobat Reader on your computer. Adobe Acrobat Reader is a program that allows you to view and print documents stored in the PDF file format. PDF stands for Portable Document Format and is a compact, cross-platform file format developed by Adobe that allows anyone anywhere to open, view, and print documents created with virtually any program on any kind of computer. The Acrobat Reader program that is installed with PhotoDeluxe only lets you view and print these files. To create your own PDF files, you will need to purchase the full Acrobat program.

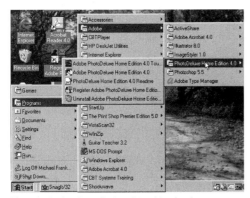

Figure 1.6 After installation, it's a bit of a chore to locate and launch PhotoDeluxe from the Start menu.

Starting and Exiting PhotoDeluxe

With the exception of being buried deep in the Start menu, Adobe PhotoDeluxe behaves just like any other Windows application when it comes to starting and exiting the program. Once you get *inside* PhotoDeluxe, it's definitely a horse of a different color, but more on that later (in Chapter 2, *PhotoDeluxe Fundamentals*, to be precise).

To start PhotoDeluxe:

1. From the Windows desktop, click on the Start button.

2. Click Programs.

3. Click Adobe.

4. Click PhotoDeluxe Home Edition 4.0.

5. Click the Adobe PhotoDeluxe Home Edition 4.0 command to actually launch the program (**Figure 1.6**).

To exit PhotoDeluxe:

◆ From the File menu, choose the Exit command.
   After all that work to get here, this seems too easy.

✔ Tip

■ Even though it is now a Windows-only program, PhotoDeluxe still retains some of its Macintosh roots. Specifically, you can use the Ctrl-Q keyboard shortcut to exit the program. This keyboard shortcut is left over from the Macintosh's Quit command (the equivalent of Windows' Exit command).

Using a shortcut

When you install PhotoDeluxe, a shortcut to the program is created on your desktop. Using this shortcut is a lot faster than climbing through the Start menu.

Unfortunately, we have so many programs on our computer that desktop shortcuts seem to breed like rabbits. We recommend doing one of two things:

◆ Create a folder on the desktop to store all of your shortcuts. Use the list view for this folder so that your shortcuts take up less screen real estate.

   or

◆ If you are using Internet Explorer 4.0's Active Desktop feature, you can drag the shortcut to the quick-launch area of the Taskbar and then delete it from the desktop completely.

PHOTODELUXE FUNDAMENTALS

For many people, the world of computer graphics is as bizarre and bewildering as it is cool and beautiful. Most of the bewilderment comes from the vast array of new concepts and terminology inherent when you apply technology to an area as diverse as art. Most of the bizarreness, coolness, and beauty comes from the art itself and the artists who create it.

This chapter introduces you to several important graphics concepts and provides a good fundamental understanding of PhotoDeluxe's environment and workflow.

Understanding the World of Graphics

All graphic images fall into one of two categories: vector-based or pixel-based. Vector-based images are created with drawing programs such as Adobe Illustrator or Macromedia FreeHand. These images consist of clean lines and discrete objects, such as logos, maps, and illustrations. Pixel-based images are created with painting programs such as Adobe Photoshop or MetaCreations Painter. They generally look much more like traditional paintings or altered photographs.

Pixel-based images can also be created by scanning an existing image, such as a photograph. When you scan in a photo, the computer reads the information and displays dots (or pixels) on your computer screen. The process of scanning in a photo is also called digitizing. When you see your photo at full size, the pixels are invisible because they are so small that they blend into each other. If you view the photo at a higher magnification, you can see the individual pixels (**Figure 2.1**).

Resolution is the number of pixels (dots on your screen) per inch (known as ppi). The higher the resolution, the clearer the image will be. When you scan in the photo, you set the resolution you want with your scanning software. The resolution also determines the size of the file. A high-resolution photo will create a larger file than a low-resolution photo. For example, at 72 ppi, an image contains 5,184 (72 x 72) pixels per square inch. At 300 ppi, the same image contains 90,000 pixels per square inch (300 x 300). For a 5 x 7 photograph, that means 181,440 pixels for a 72 ppi scan versus 3,150,000 pixels for a 300 ppi scan!

Figure 2.1 The higher the magnification, the larger individual pixels become.

For photos meant to be used on a Web page, your resolution need not be any higher than 72 pixels per inch since all monitors only display at 72 ppi. This is also true for photos used in on-screen presentations. However, for photos or other images intended for printing, you should use a higher resolution (although more than 300 ppi is probably not necessary unless you will be doing *very* detailed work on the image). 150 ppi is probably adequate for most desktop printers, but if you are going to be outputting to a professional printer, use higher resolutions. Better yet, talk to your printer *before* scanning or creating your images. He or she can tell you all about the wonders of line screens, dot gain, color separations, and more!

UNDERSTANDING THE WORLD OF GRAPHICS

Understanding Scanners, Photo-CDs, and Digital Cameras

Scanners, photo-CDs, and digital cameras are three great ways to add to your library of images. Each has its uses and drawbacks, but they are all worth looking into if you plan on doing a lot of work with PhotoDeluxe or other image-editing applications.

The only way to work with existing photos is to have them scanned. Scanning an image creates a digital version of that image, which can then be manipulated using an image-editing program (like, say, PhotoDeluxe, for example). You can take an image to a service bureau or print shop and have them scan it onto a disk for you, but a far better solution is to buy a scanner and do it yourself. Low-end scanners cost anywhere from $80 to $300. For about $120-$180 you can get yourself a good scanner (we like HP and UMAX scanners, personally) that will do everything you need. If you are planning on doing a lot of scanning, we recommend getting a scanner with either a SCSI or USB interface. Scanners that use a parallel interface are much slower than SCSI or USB models.

Photo-CDs are becoming a very popular way to access a multitude of photos. Commercial photo-CDs can be ordered through computer magazines or bought at your nearest computer store. The photos that come on the CD are usually royalty free, meaning that you can use them freely in your own artistic endeavors. Another type of photo-CD is one that you have created yourself from a roll of your own film. You take your pictures as you normally would, but when you have them developed, have them saved onto a photo-CD instead of (or in addition to) having prints made. This saves you the trouble of scanning the images in manually, and generally results in cleaner, sharper digital files.

A digital camera is a great way to by-pass the film development process entirely. With a digital camera, you can take pictures and access them from PhotoDeluxe without scanning or using a photo-CD. The only real drawbacks to digital cameras are their cost ($400 to $1000 or more) and their limited resolution. For example, most digital cameras capture an image using 640 by 480 pixels. This means that one picture could fill your screen (at 72 ppi) and look great, but that same image would have to be reduced considerably in size to give you acceptable quality when printed (remember, printed images need much higher resolution than on-screen images). Our recommendation is to use a digital camera only if your final destination is an on-screen image (such as a Web site). Using a traditional camera and scanning the images yourself lets you choose the resolution you need.

Scanning Images

Because most people will be getting their images into PhotoDeluxe using traditional film and then scanning their images, there are a few dos and don'ts to keep in mind when it comes to scanning.

Do

◆ Start with good images. You will always lose at least a little bit of image quality when scanning, so make sure you start with the best images you can get.

◆ Make sure the image and the scanner glass are clean. It's amazing to us that people who are willing to spend hours cleaning up a file in Photoshop or PhotoDeluxe aren't willing to spend two minutes to do a good job cleaning their scanner. We recommend spraying glass cleaner on a clean, lint-free cloth or quality paper towel, then wiping down the scanner glass. Never spray any liquid onto the scanner itself, as excess can leak into the scanner. This also goes for cleaning your monitor.

◆ Scan at the highest resolution you think you will need. You can safely lower the resolution of an image once it is in your computer, but you can't increase the resolution and keep your image entirely intact.

Don't

◆ Be in a hurry. Set up your image precisely and scan it as many times as it takes to get it right.

◆ Scan different image types together. You will generally be better off scanning your photos with your scanner set one way, then doing a separate scan for text and line art.

◆ Run with scissors.

Copyright and Copywrong

Copyright laws protect the artist or publisher of an image. What this means to you and me is that when a piece of art is copyrighted, we cannot in any way use the whole or even a portion of the image, unless granted written permission by the original artist or publisher. This is true whether or not a piece of art is labeled with a copyright symbol. When you purchase a CD with a collection of photos, you have to check the licensing agreement regarding how many times you can use the images. Some of the CD collections allow unlimited use of the images. The best rule of thumb is if you are wondering about a certain image, don't use it. If you really want to use a copyrighted image, write or e-mail the artist or publisher for permission. Quite often, artists will happily give you permission for single, non-commercial usage. The main objection from artists we know isn't that people want to re-use their work, it's that people want to re-use their work without permission or acknowledgment.

Using Sample Images and Clip Art

PhotoDeluxe comes with a wide variety of sample images and clip art. These allow you to experiment with different effects even if you don't have any appropriate photos of your own, or you can add these images and clip art to your own photos to create fun or interesting collages and special effects.

The samples can easily be accessed from within PhotoDeluxe or almost any image-editing application, but they do require that you have the PhotoDeluxe CD in your CD-ROM drive. (Because of how much room they take up, these images and clip art are not included in a standard installation of PhotoDeluxe.)

By the way, you certainly aren't limited to just using the sample images and clip art that come with PhotoDeluxe. Just about any photo sample or clip art can be used, as long as it is stored in a file format that PhotoDeluxe recognizes. For example, you can use your Microsoft Office clip art with PhotoDeluxe, as long as you convert it from PICT format to a format PhotoDeluxe can read, such as BMP or TIFF. Of course, to do this conversion, you will need a program (such as Photoshop) that understands both PICT and BMP or TIFF file formats.

Also, you will not be able to access "foreign" clip art the same way you do PhotoDeluxe's clip art. Instead, you will need to open the file from disk, as explained in Chapter 3, *Getting Images into PhotoDeluxe*.

Learning the PhotoDeluxe Interface

PhotoDeluxe has an interface and workflow that are unique among software programs (at least, among all of the software programs we've seen).

The PhotoDeluxe interface consists of a large work area where your images are displayed (**Figure 2.2**). To the left of this area is a scrolling list of image thumbnails. Above the work area is the "activity bar" with bright, colorful buttons that start you on any one of dozens of guided activities (as discussed in Chapters 4 through 6).

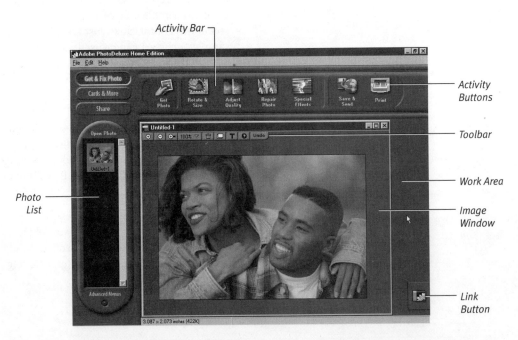

Figure 2.2 The PhotoDeluxe interface.

Within the work area you'll find individual windows for each image that you currently have open. Each of these windows has its own toolbar (**Figure 2.3**) which contains buttons for increasing or decreasing magnification, erasing and rearranging images or sections of images, adding text, accessing the help system, and undoing actions.

You also have pop-out buttons along the right border for linking to various Web sites to access additional image-editing resources.

These pages illustrate all of these PhotoDeluxe interface elements. Please take some time to familiarize yourself with the locations of all the various buttons, bars, tools, and menus shown here, as we'll be referring to them throughout the book.

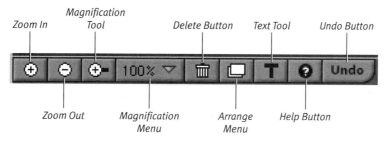

Figure 2.3 The toolbar within an image window.

LEARNING THE PHOTODELUXE INTERFACE

Following Guided Activities

Most of the tasks you will need to perform can be accomplished by simply following along with an appropriate guided activity. Guided activities are discussed in detail in Chapters 4 through 6, but it will help you understand the underlying philosophy of PhotoDeluxe if we take a look at how guided activities work.

Note that guided activities only work if you have an image open, so we'll begin by opening a sample image. Chapter 3 covers all the ways you can get images into PhotoDeluxe.

To use a guided activity:

1. If necessary, click on the Get & Fix Photo tab (in the upper-left corner of the PhotoDeluxe interface).

2. Click the Get Photo button.

   One thing that might take a little getting used to is that PhotoDeluxe buttons don't look like buttons at all. Instead, they just look like pictures on the screen. However, when you point to one of these pictures, a glow will surround it, which lets you know that it is something to click on.

3. From the resulting pop-up menu, click the Free Stuff command.

4. Click the Sample Photos command in the Free Stuff submenu. The Samples palette appears.

5. Drag any image in the Samples palette into the work area (**Figure 2.4**).

6. Close the Samples palette.

   As with any Windows window, you can simply click the X in the upper-right corner.

7. Now that you have an image open, click Rotate & Size in the activity bar.

Figure 2.4 Dragging an image from the palette to the work area imports the image.

Figure 2.5 Guided activities always lead you step-by-step through a task.

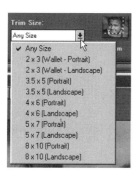

Figure 2.6 This pop-up list has all of the standard photo sizes you will need.

Figure 2.7 A tab with advice and commentary pops up as you work on your tasks.

Figure 2.8
This bounding box is the size you selected from the pop-up list. Move it to trim your image.

8. From the resulting Rotate & Size menu, select Trim & Size.

This takes us to the standard look we'll see whenever we are following a guided activity (**Figure 2.5**).

9. Click the Trim tab at the top of the activity bar.

10. From the Trim Size list, select a size (**Figure 2.6**).

A sometimes helpful/sometimes annoying comment tab pops up along the right side of the work area (**Figure 2.7**). Click on it to make it go away.

11. Click the Trim button, as prompted.

12. Drag the bounding box over the part of the image you want to keep.

The term "bounding box" simply refers to a box which defines or outlines the boundaries of a selected image, image portion, or image element (such as text). By dragging or resizing this box, you can usually move, rotate, or stretch your image. In this case, the bounding box is being used to select a portion of a larger image.

You can continue to close the comment tab each time it pops up, or just leave it up on-screen.

13. Click outside of the bounding box to complete the trimming process (**Figure 2.8**).

14. Click the Done tab to exit the activity.

FOLLOWING GUIDED ACTIVITIES

✔ Tip

■ It is important to note that the OK and Cancel buttons in the activity bar during a guided activity generally refer to the specific portion of the activity that you are currently in, not to the entire activity. That is, if you click the OK or Cancel buttons while positioning the trim bounding box, you only confirm or cancel the bounding box placement, not the entire trim activity. If you change your mind and wish to exit out of the activity completely, simply cancel any change you may have made, then click the Done tab.

Simple Selections

Many guided activities will have you making selections in an image. While there are lots of ways to select in PhotoDeluxe, most of them are only available when you are using the advanced menus. During guided activities, you will make selections by either drawing a rectangular selection area around the part of the image you wish to select or you will use a "smart selection" tool.

The smart selection tool has a "magnetic" effect that causes it to follow along a portion of the image based on color values. For example, if you want to select a cloud against a blue sky with this tool, you simply click on the edge of the cloud and move to another point along the edge. As you move the cursor (don't press and drag—you simply click on different edge points) the selection will hug the edge of the cloud. This takes a little getting used to, but it is the easiest way to make a non-rectangular selection. For more information on this smart selection tool, see Chapter 9, *Selection Techniques*.

FOLLOWING GUIDED ACTIVITIES

GETTING IMAGES INTO PHOTODELUXE

We are sure it will come as no surprise to anyone that before you can use PhotoDeluxe to manipulate an image, you must first get the image *into* PhotoDeluxe. There are many ways to do this, from simply opening a file from disk to working through a multi-step guided activity to retrieve an image from a digital camera or scanner.

All of the techniques used to get an image into PhotoDeluxe can be found in the Get Photo pop-up menu in the Get & Fix Photo activity bar.

Retrieving an Image from My Photos

PhotoDeluxe has a great feature for storing and retrieving images: Albums. Albums are palettes containing thumbnails of all of your saved images. The My Photos album is the default album when you save a file, and it's a quick and easy way to retrieve images you want to work with.

Note: Saving images into an album (such as My Photos) is discussed in Chapter 7, *Saving and Exporting Images*.

To retrieve an image from My Photos:

1. Click Get Photo in the activity bar.

2. From the pop-up menu, select My Photos (**Figure 3.1**).

   The My Photos album appears at the bottom of the work area.

3. Scroll through the thumbnails to find the image you want to use.

   If you haven't saved any images into the My Photos album, you can click on the Album button and use a sample image.

4. Drag the thumbnail of the desired image out of the album and into the work area.

   The full-size version of the image appears in the work area and a thumbnail appears in the Open Photos list (**Figure 3.2**).

5. Close the album window.

Figure 3.1 The My Photos command gives you access to all images stored in the My Photos album.

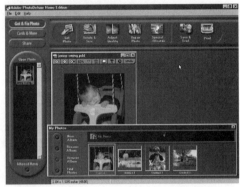

Figure 3.2 Dragging a thumbnail out of the album and into the work area opens the file that the thumbnail represents.

Figure 3.3 The preview at the bottom of this Open dialog box is invaluable if you work with lots of files.

Opening a File

If you want to open an image that has not already been saved into a PhotoDeluxe album, you can simply open the file from disk, just as you would open any file in any Windows application. This is how you would open a file from a floppy disk, a CD-ROM, a removable cartridge (such as a Zip disk), over a network, or previously stored on your hard drive.

To open a file on a disk:

1. Click Get Photo in the activity bar.

2. From the pop-up menu, select Open File.

   You will be presented with a slightly modified Windows Open dialog box. This dialog box includes a handy preview area at the bottom (**Figure 3.3**).

   You can also simply choose the Open command from the File menu to access this dialog box.

3. Navigate through the dialog box to locate and select the file that you want to open.

4. Once the file is selected, simply click the Open button to open it.

Connecting to a Digital Camera

In our opinion, a digital camera is one of the coolest high-tech toys you can own. Its ability to capture and immediately display images makes it great fun at parties and family gatherings, and there is no easier way to get images into PhotoDeluxe or other graphics software programs. On the down side, the resolution of the images is generally low, so they are best suited for images that will never be printed or will only be printed at small sizes.

To get files from a digital camera:

1. Click Get Photo in the activity bar.

2. Select Cameras from the pop-up menu.

3. Click the Camera tab.

4. Select your camera model from the pop-up Camera Models menu (**Figure 3.4**).

5. Click Open Camera to the right of the pop-up menu. Depending on your camera software, the dialog box you get may look different. We used a Fuji MX-700 digital camera to take this "behind the scenes" picture of the writer hard at work.

6. Make sure that your camera is on and properly connected to your computer, then click the appropriate button in the dialog box to capture the image you want. In this case, we simply pointed the camera at the monitor and clicked the camera button (**Figure 3.5**).

7. Click the acquire/download/transfer button (depending on what your camera software calls it) to transfer the image data to your computer and into PhotoDeluxe (**Figure 3.6**).

8. Click the Done tab in the activity bar.

Figure 3.4 This list shows all digital camera drivers installed on your computer.

Figure 3.5 The Fuji MX 700 camera supports this very cool "live" picture feature.

Figure 3.6 The final picture in PhotoDeluxe. The big feet are included for their aesthetic value. We are, after all, artists.

✔ Tip

■ Not all cameras support this "live" feature. Depending on your camera and the software it came with, your only option may be to select from a list of images already stored in your camera.

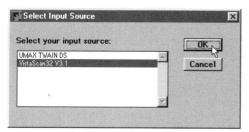

Figure 3.7 Choose your scanning software.

Figure 3.8 PhotoDeluxe's guided scanning steps.

Figure 3.9 Using the scanner manufacturer's software to scan an image (in this case, UMAX's VistaScan).

Scanning an Image

Scanning images is the most common method for getting images into PhotoDeluxe. Not only does scanning allow you to decide on the quality of your image (lower quality for screen display, higher for printing), but it is the only way to use all of those photos from the old family albums.

When you scan an image, you can use either the PhotoDeluxe interface or you can switch to your scanner's software, giving you more control and scanning options.

To scan an image into PhotoDeluxe:

1. Click the Get Photo button in the Get & Fix Photo activity bar.

2. Select the Scanners command from the pop-up menu.

3. Click the Scanner tab.

4. Click the Choose Scanner button.

5. From the Select Input Source dialog box, select the scanning software that you want to use (**Figure 3.7**) and click OK.

6. Click the Mode tab.

7. Click the Guided or Custom button to select your scanning mode.

   Guided mode walks you through additional PhotoDeluxe steps to scan the image (**Figure 3.8**).

   Custom mode lets you use your scanner's software to scan the image (**Figure 3.9**).

8. Click the Done tab once you are finished scanning.

Using the Free Stuff

Like most reasonably sane human beings, we really like free stuff. PhotoDeluxe comes with a bunch of free stuff, including dozens of sample photos to experiment with or use in your compositions, clip art to spice up cards, calendars and more, and one of the niftiest ideas we've seen in a long time—Changeables. Sample photos and clip art need no explanation, and Changeables are best seen to be understood, but you can think of Changeables as clip art with a twist—sliders that let you control all sorts of parameters such as shape, size, color, and style.

To use sample photos:

1. Click the Get Photo button in the Get & Fix Photo activity bar.

2. Select Free Stuff > Sample Photos from the pop-up menu.

3. The Sample Photos window appears. Click any button at the top of the Sample Photos window to view different albums.

4. Drag the desired photo from the album to the work area to open the file (**Figure 3.10**). That's all there is to it.

To use clip art:

1. Click the Get Photo button in the Get & Fix Photo activity bar.

2. Select Free Stuff > Clip Art from the pop-up menu.

3. The Clip Art window appears (**Figure 3.11**).
   Click any button at the top of the Clip Art window to view different albums of clip art.

4. Drag the desired image from the album to the work area to open and work with the file.

Figure 3.10 The Sample Photos album.

Figure 3.11 The Clip Art album.

Figure 3.12 Using the sliders in the Changeable dialog box, you can create hundreds of variations of the same piece of Changeables artwork.

To use Changeables:

1. Click the Get Photo button in the Get & Fix Photo activity bar.

2. Select Free Stuff > Changeables from the pop-up menu.

3. Drag the desired image from the gallery to the work area.

   With Changeables, you have a chance to alter the image before it is placed in the work area. You can go back and alter it further at any time by simply double-clicking on the image.

4. Drag the sliders in the Changeable dialog box to alter the color, style, dimensions, and other parameters of the image (**Figure 3.12**).

5. Click the OK button to close the dialog box and apply your changes.

USING THE FREE STUFF

PART 2

GUIDED ACTIVITIES

Guided Activities

Probably the most distinguishing feature of PhotoDeluxe is its task-oriented approach to enhancing images and creating art. Whereas most programs just give you a bunch of tools, PhotoDeluxe focuses on guided activities, walking you step-by-step through the process of retouching a photo, creating a greeting card, or printing a calendar.

The PhotoDeluxe activity bar, which is the focus of Part 2 of this book, is divided into three sections, each of which corresponds to a different set of guided activities:

The **Get & Fix Photo** button is used to bring images into PhotoDeluxe for manipulation or inclusion in other works. The process of opening or importing images is discussed in detail in Chapter 3, *Getting Images into PhotoDeluxe*. In this section, you will use the "Fix Photo" part of the Get & Fix Photo guided activities to rotate, trim, and resize photos, make color and tonal adjustments, remove unwanted elements or repair damaged photos, and apply artistic or just plain bizarre special effects to images.

The **Cards & More** button is used to create all sorts of printed material by combining your images with pre-designed templates. By following these guided activities you will be able to create customized greeting and holiday cards, monthly and yearly calendars, photo album pages, frames, and more.

Lastly, the **Share** button lets you share images over the Internet using Adobe's ActiveShare Web site, with e-mail, or by creating custom Web projects. You can also take advantage of the extensibility of PhotoDeluxe by downloading and using guided activities for topical events such as holidays and different seasons.

MODIFYING IMAGES

The first set of guided activities involves making modifications to the original image. These modifications can be as simple as trimming away unwanted parts of the image, or as complex as restoring an old photograph to look like new.

All guided activities work in approximately the same way: Start the activity, click each tab in succession, and complete the task required in each tab, whether it be making a selection, zooming in to a specific image location, or adjusting settings in a dialog box.

Many of the changes you'll be making in this chapter are highly subjective, so use the Undo button in the image window to toggle between the effect and the original image, deciding for yourself if the change helped or hurt the image.

Note: Refer to the color section to see several before-and-after examples of images that were fixed using the techniques described in this chapter.

Rotating, Flipping, and Trimming Images

The simplest modifications you can make to an image are rotations, flips, and trims. Rotating or flipping an image is simply a matter of selecting the appropriate command from a menu. Trimming is a little more involved, but not much.

The term trimming is synonymous with "cropping," which is what professional digital artists call it. In this example we used a holiday greeting card we received (**Figure 4.1**), flipping it over and trimming away the greeting and the names.

Figure 4.1 This incredibly cute postcard could, with some minor fixes, be used for a lot of different purposes.

To rotate or flip an image:

1. Click Rotate & Size in the activity bar.

2. Select Rotate Left, Rotate Right, Flip Horizontal or Flip Vertical from the pop-up menu.
   Rotate Left turns the image 90 degrees counter-clockwise.
   Rotate Right turns the image 90 degrees clockwise.
   Flip Horizontal mirrors the image left to right (**Figure 4.2**).
   Flip Vertical mirrors the image top to bottom.

Figure 4.2 A simple flip puts the oldest girl on the left-hand side of the image.

To trim an image:

1. Click Rotate & Size in the activity bar.

2. Select Trim & Size from the pop-up menu.

3. Click the Trim tab in the activity bar.

4. If you want a standard size, such as a 2 x 3 wallet, select the desired size from the Trim Size pop-up list.

5. Click the Trim button.

Figure 4.3 With the holiday greeting trimmed away, this image is ready to go.

6. If you selected a standard size, drag within the bounding box to frame the part of the image that you want to keep.

7. If you did not select a standard size, press and drag to define a rectangular bounding box around the part of the image that you want to keep.

8. Click the green OK checkmark to trim away the unwanted part of the image (**Figure 4.3**).

If you make a mistake when moving or creating the bounding box, simply click the red Cancel button to redefine the boundary.

9. Click the Done tab.

Using Extensis Instant Fix Tools

Extensis is a small company (at least, compared to Adobe) that makes some really useful software. One of their many products is Intellihance (for *intelligent enhancement*), which, in a very modified form, is included in PhotoDeluxe as IntelliFix.

The best things about the Extensis instant fixes is that they are, well, instant. Play around with any of them, especially the Instant Fix itself, and you will wonder how you ever did without them.

To instantly fix an image:

1. Make sure the Get & Fix Photo button at the left of the activity bar is selected.

2. Click the Adjust Quality button.

3. Select Extensis Instant Fix Tools from the pop-up menu.

4. From the Extensis sub-menu, select IntelliFix™ Instant Fix (**Figure 4.4**).

    As you might guess, this command instantly fixes many potential problem areas in the image, such as brightness, contrast, and color balance. In fact, we tend to always use Instant Fix on our images, if only to compare the "fixed" image to the original and see which we like better.

5. Click the Undo button in the image window (**Figure 4.5**) to compare the before and after images.

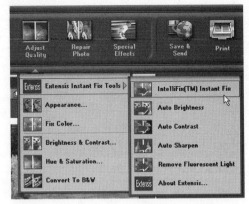

Figure 4.4 The Extensis instant fixes are incredibly useful.

Figure 4.5 You can use the Undo button as a toggle between an applied fix and the original image.

To selectively apply instant fixes:

1. Click the Adjust Quality button in the Get & Fix Photo activity bar.

2. Click the Extensis Instant Fix Tools command.

3. Select the Auto Brightness, Auto Contrast, Auto Sharpen, or Remove Fluorescent Light command, depending on what aspect of your image needs fixing.

   Auto Brightness increases the brightness of your image, lightening dark areas and revealing many details hidden in shadow.

   Auto Contrast increases the contrast of your image. Contrast is the difference between the light and dark areas of your image.

   Auto Sharpen increases the definition of your image, making blurry or indistinct photos much clearer.

   Remove Fluorescent Light removes the greenish-yellow cast that often results from taking photographs of subjects under fluorescent light.

4. Click the Undo button in the image window to compare the before and after images.

Adjusting Image Appearance

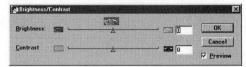

Figure 4.6 The Brightness and Contrast dialog box.

The Appearance guided activity is not so much an activity in itself as it is a combination of several other guided activities, bundled into one sequence. This may be the only activity you use to fix photographs. Once you know your needs better, you may then skip this combination activity and just run the single (and thus, shorter) activity to fix the one aspect of your photo that needs fixing.

The Fix Color guided activity is different from most other activities in that you pick from different pre-defined samples of your photo, rather than manually adjust the amount of an effect that you pick. It is a less precise, but ultimately satisfying way to change the overall color of your photograph.

To change the overall appearance of an image:

1. Click the Adjust Quality button in the Get & Fix Photo activity bar.

2. Select the Appearance command.

3. Click the Instant Fix tab.

4. Click the Instant Fix button.
   Applying an Instant Fix is usually a good first step when working on an image.

5. Click the Tune tab.

6. Click the Brightness & Contrast button.
   The Brightness/Contrast dialog box appears.

7. Drag the Brightness and Contrast sliders to make adjustments to your image (**Figure 4.6**).

8. When you are happy with the changes you've made, click the OK button.

9. Click the Adjust tab.

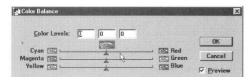

Figure 4.7 The Color Balance dialog box.

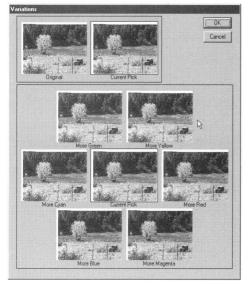

Figure 4.8 The Variations dialog box lets you shift your colors in any direction and as much as you want.

10. Click the Color Balance button.
    The Color Balance dialog box appears.

11. Drag the Cyan/Red, Magenta/Green and Yellow/Blue sliders to adjust the color balance of your image (Figure 4.7).

12. Click the OK button when you are done.

13. Click the Done tab.

To fix image color with Variations:

1. Click the Adjust Quality button in the activity bar.

2. Select Fix Color from the pop-up menu.

3. Click the Variations tab.

4. Click the Variations button.

5. In the Variations dialog box (Figure 4.8) click on any of the variations (More Yellow, More Red, etc.) of your current pick.

   Continue clicking on variations until you are happy with the color. You can start over again at any time by clicking the original image in the upper-left corner of the dialog box.

6. Click the OK button to apply these changes to your image.

ADJUSTING IMAGE APPEARANCE

Fine-tuning the Image

The Appearance guided activity is great for images with a lot of problems, since it lets you adjust many different aspects of the image. However, if you only need to correct one or two image problems (such as increasing brightness or tweaking color tint) you can just go straight to either the Brightness & Contrast or Hue & Saturation activities, both of which can be found in the Adjust Quality button pop-up menu. These activities let you fine-tune your image with remarkable precision.

Note: If you want to convert a color image to black and white, you can either use the Convert to B & W activity or manually reduce the saturation of your image to –100 (which will remove all color) in the Hue & Saturation activity.

To manually adjust brightness and contrast:

1. Click the Adjust Quality button and select the Brightness & Contrast command.

   The Brightness/Contrast dialog box appears.

2. Drag the Brightness and Contrast sliders to modify your image (**Figure 4.9**).

3. Click the OK button when you are done.

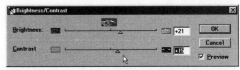

Figure 4.9 This is the same Brightness and Contrast dialog box used in one of the steps of the Appearance command.

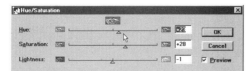

Figure 4.10 These three sliders let you control color value, color amount, and the amount of black or white in an image.

To manually adjust hue and saturation:

1. Click the Adjust Quality button and select the Hue & Saturation command. The Hue/Saturation dialog box appears.

2. Drag the Hue, Saturation, and Lightness sliders to modify your image (**Figure 4.10**).

   The Hue slider is not really a "more or less" slider like the others that we have seen to this point. Hue is a cyclical value, wherein the slider actually "wraps" around so that the opposite edges of the slider meet. Dragging the Hue slider all the way to the left or all the way to the right produces the same result, so you really just drag the slider to decide where along the color spectrum you want your image to fall.

   The Saturation slider adjusts the amount of color in the image. Dragging the slider all the way to the left turns your image into a black and white photo, while dragging the slider to the right over-saturates the image with color.

   The Lightness slider increases the amount of black or white in your image. Dragging the slider all the way to the left gives you a pure black image, while dragging all the way to the right gives you a pure white image. Both extremes are, obviously, fairly pointless.

3. Click the OK button when you are done.

FINE-TUNING THE IMAGE

Restoring and Retouching Photos

The technique used for restoring or retouching photographs is the same. Restoring usually refers to fixing physical damage to photographs, especially old photographs, whereas retouching can be anything from erasing a blemish from a face to removing a plane or power lines from an otherwise perfect sky.

In addition, the process of restoring old photos usually involves steps other than pure retouching. Many old photos will need to have significant color correction work, at the very least.

To retouch a photo:

1. Click the Repair Photo button in the Get & Fix Photo activity bar.

2. Select any of these commands: Remove Elements, Retouch Face, or Restore Old Photo (**Figure 4.11**).

   All three activities are virtually identical. The main difference is that the Remove Elements activity prompts you to erase the unwanted element first and then paint over it, which we think is a very bad idea. You will have better results simply painting over the unwanted element without first creating an ugly white hole where the element used to be (and which, incidentally, is more difficult to cover up than the original unwanted element).

3. Zoom in to the unwanted element.

   You can click the Zoom tab (if you are using either the Retouch Face or Restore Old Photo activity) and click the Zoom button there, or just use the zoom tools in the image window.

4. Click the Cover tab (for the Remove Elements activity) or the Repair tab

Figure 4.11 The Remove Elements activity is very similar to the Retouch Face and Restore Old Photo activities.

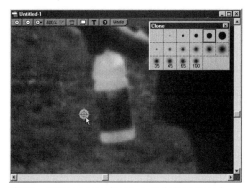

Figure 4.12 Zoom in to the unwanted element and select an area to clone from.

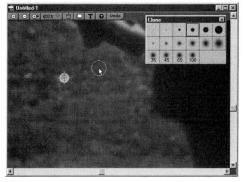

Figure 4.13 Paint over the unwanted element to replace it with another portion of the image.

(for the Retouch Face or Restore Old Photo activities).

5. Click the Clone button.

    A crosshair-shaped sampling point appears on the image.

6. Drag the sampling point to an area that looks the way you want the unwanted portion of your image to look (**Figure 4.12**).

7. Paint (press and drag) over the unwanted portion of your image to replace it based on the image under the sampling point (**Figure 4.13**).

✔ Tip

- When cloning like this, it is a good idea to use several different sampling points. This prevents the obvious repetition of another image area. Also remember that you can pick different brush sizes for more detailed work.

RESTORING AND RETOUCHING PHOTOS

Removing Red Eye

We once owned a very expensive camera whose manufacturer seemed to have confused the concept of red eye reduction with red eye enhancement. Every picture we took was sharp and clear and gorgeous, except for the demonic red eyes of the people in the pictures. And we aren't talking about a red *tint*, we're talking about deep, rich, practically glowing red eyes. While we never did figure out exactly what the problem with that camera was, we now know that should we run into that problem again, PhotoDeluxe can come to the rescue. Red eye reduction is one of the most common uses for PhotoDeluxe and is often (and justifiably) the main reason for purchasing the software.

To remove red eye from a photo:

1. Click the Repair Photo button in the Get & Fix Photo activity bar.

2. Select Remove Red Eye from the pop-up menu.

3. Click the Select tab.

4. Click the Select Rectangle button and drag a rectangle around the eyes of your photo (**Figure 4.14**).

5. Click the Remove tab.

6. Click the Remove Red Eye button.

7. You may need to click this button more than once before all of the red is removed. This is especially true at higher resolutions, such as in the sample image (**Figure 4.15**).

   We've found that it is sometimes better to remove the red eye manually, using the advanced techniques discussed in Chapter 14, *Correcting Image Problems*.

8. Click the Done tab.

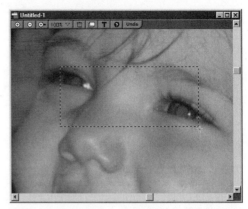

Figure 4.14 Select just the eyes, or PhotoDeluxe may remove some red from other parts of your photo.

Figure 4.15 After four applications of red eye removal, this image is acceptable.

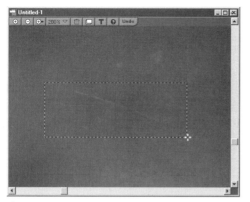

Figure 4.16 Removing dust and scratches should be done conservatively and to small image areas only, as with this selection of a small scratch.

Removing Dust, Scratches, and Noise

These days, with digital cameras, video cameras, photo CDs, and scanners, you have a lot of choices about how to capture and preserve those special moments for posterity. In the old days, though, all you had was film, photographs, and shoe boxes. And shoe boxes, while inexpensive and readily available, aren't known for their ability to protect their contents from dust, scratches, squishing, dropping, dripping, or drenching. Because of this, many of us have old photos with minor or major damage. Major damage can sometimes be repaired using the retouching techniques discussed earlier, but minor damage such as small scratches, dust on the scan, or noise (tiny, random patterns of dots) from a poor image or scan, can be cleaned up using the following techniques.

To remove dust or scratches from a photo:

1. Click the Repair Photo button in the Get & Fix Photo activity bar.

2. Select Remove Dust & Scratches from the pop-up menu.

3. Click the Select tab.

4. Click the Select Rectangle button and drag a rectangle around the area you want to fix.

   It is best to fix just the portions of the image that contain the dust or scratches. Dust and scratches are removed by blending adjacent image pixels, so some image quality is lost in the clean-up process. Therefore, try not to apply this effect to large portions of your image. We recommend zooming in to at least 200% or more when using this effect (**Figure 4.16**).

(continues on next page)

REMOVING DUST, SCRATCHES, AND NOISE

5. Click the Dust & Scratches tab.

6. Click the Dust & Scratches button in the activity bar.

7. In the Dust & Scratches dialog box, drag the Radius and Threshold sliders until the scratches or dust are no longer visible.

To avoid obvious changes to the selected area, use the lowest possible settings that will successfully remove the dust or scratches.

8. Click the OK button.

9. Click the Done tab.

To remove noise from a photo:

1. Click the Repair Photo button in the Get & Fix Photo activity bar.

2. Select Remove Noise from the pop-up menu.

3. Click the tab that corresponds to the type of noise you want to remove.

Graininess is good for poor-quality scans or scans of poor-quality images, such as those from newspapers.

Moire is good for images that display moiré patterns, which can also result from a bad scan or from poor image manipulation.

JPEG is useful when JPEG-compressed images have unsightly blocks of color instead of smooth gradations.

4. Click the Reduce Graininess, Remove Moire, or Clean Up JPEG button (depending on which tab you clicked in the previous step).

5. Adjust the slider in the dialog box for the type of noise you want to remove (**Figure 4.17**).

Figure 4.17 Removing graininess should also be done conservatively, but is generally applied to the entire image.

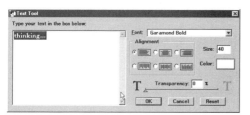

Figure 4.18 The Text Tool dialog box lets you change all of the standard text attributes, as well as transparency!

Figure 4.19 One text object added to the original image.

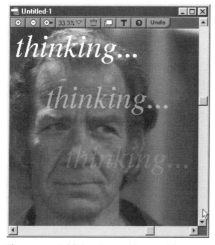

Figure 4.20 Additional text objects, with increasing amounts of transparency added.

Adding Text

A picture may be worth a thousand words, but a word or two can sure make a picture worth even more. PhotoDeluxe handles text very simply, allowing you to add as much text as you want over your image, and to reposition, resize, and rotate it with ease. You can even make your text partially or fully transparent! (Although fully transparent text would be kind of pointless.)

To add text to an image:

1. Click the Special Effects button in the Get & Fix Photo activity bar.

2. Select Add Text from the pop-up menu.

3. In the Text Tool dialog box (**Figure 4.18**), type your text in the space along the left side.

4. Change the font, alignment, size, and color of the text, as desired.

5. Click OK.

   Your text is added to your image (**Figure 4.19**). Drag the middle of the text to move it, or drag the handles to resize it.

   If you want, repeat these steps to add additional text to your image, experimenting with the Transparency slider to create see-through text (**Figure 4.20**). You can also double-click on your existing text to edit it.

ADDING TEXT

Applying Special Effects

Be prepared to lose hours or even whole days fooling around with all of the cool special effects that you can create with PhotoDeluxe. In this section, we only show you one of the 41 different effects available. Because there are so many, we have dedicated an entire chapter (Chapter 13, to be precise) to special effects.

To apply special effects to an image:

1. Click the Special Effects button in the Get & Fix Photo activity bar.

2. Select the desired special effect from the pop-up menu (**Figure 4.21**).

   For this example, we will use the Impression special effect from the Artistic sub-menu.

3. Click through the tabs at the top of the activity bar to step through the special effect you have chosen.

4. Use the sliders in any dialog boxes you are presented with to adjust the effect's settings (**Figure 4.22**).

5. Click the Done tab when you are happy with the results (**Figure 4.23**).

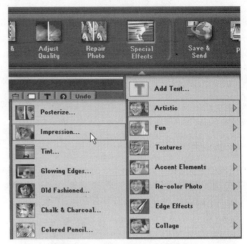

Figure 4.21 This is just one of the 41 different special effects in PhotoDeluxe!

Figure 4.22 Dragging the slider in the dialog box will reduce or increase the effects' effect (you know what we mean).

Figure 4.23 "Father and Daughter Fishing," an original work in the impressionist style by <insert your name here>.

CREATING CALENDARS, CARDS, AND MORE

One of the many facets of PhotoDeluxe is its ability to create composite images—images that combine multiple sources. Creating free-form composite images includes tasks such as faking a vacation photo by inserting a photo of yourself into a picture of the Taj Mahal, or creating a "horror of science" photo by digitally grafting an animal head onto a person's body. Creating these types of composite images is discussed in detail in Chapter 10, *Combining Images*. For now, we will limit our compositing to pre-designed guided activities for creating cards, calendars, signs, labels, and more by adding pictures to templates containing borders, text, and artwork.

As long as you have a color printer for output, this can be a great way to personalize holiday and birthday cards and gifts, schoolwork, mailing labels, signs, and small posters.

Creating Cards

Whether it's for a birthday or holiday or just to say "Here's the latest picture of the baby," creating and sending a personalized card makes any occasion more special. With PhotoDeluxe, you can choose from a wide variety of pre-designed template styles and include any image you want. In addition to traditional "greeting" cards and postcards, you can also create fun sports trading cards, perfect for that developing Little League or gymnastics star.

To create a greeting card or postcard:

1. Click the Cards button in the Cards & More activity bar.

2. Select Greeting Cards or Postcards from the pop-up menu.

3. Click the Layout tab to display a list of standard card layouts (**Figure 5.1**).

4. Click on the button in the activity bar that corresponds to the card layout you want to use.

5. Click the Style tab and then click the Choose Style button.

6. In the Templates palette, double-click on the card style that you want to use (**Figure 5.2**).

7. Click the View tab and read about the different view options.

8. Click the Add tab.

9. Use any of the buttons listed in the activity bar to bring an image into PhotoDeluxe.
   For detailed information about getting images into PhotoDeluxe, see Chapter 3, *Getting Images into PhotoDeluxe.* (Amazing how that works, isn't it?)

Figure 5.1 Four ways to fold a piece of paper into a greeting card.

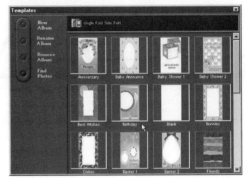

Figure 5.2 Double-click to use any of these pre-designed greeting card templates.

Figure 5.3 Use these handles to resize or rotate the image.

10. Move and resize the image so that it fits within the card opening.

    Drag the round rotation handles to rotate the image, drag the solid square handles to resize the image, and drag the middle of the image to move the image (**Figure 5.3**).

11. Click the Edit tab and read about editing options.

    We recommend editing the image as a separate activity, and then using it in a greeting card or other activity.

12. Click the Done tab.

To create a sports card:

1. Click the Cards button in the Cards & More activity bar.

2. Select Sports Cards from the pop-up menu.

3. Click the Choose Sports Card tab and then click the Choose Card button.

4. In the Templates palette, double-click on the card style that you want to use.

5. Click the Add tab.

6. Use any of the buttons listed in the activity bar to bring an image into PhotoDeluxe.

7. Move and resize the image so that it fits within the card opening.

8. Click the Edit tab and read about editing options.

9. Click the Done tab.

✔ Tip

■ Any text in the card templates can be easily replaced by simply double-clicking the existing text (which opens a text-editing dialog box) and then typing in your new text.

Creating Calendars

A personalized calendar makes a great holiday gift for friends and family. By personalizing each calendar with photos of you, the kids, or special times that you've spent with the calendar recipient, you can let everyone know how special they are to you. And by using PhotoDeluxe to create the calendar, you can do so with little time or effort. (Ha ha!) Seriously, personalized calendars are easy to create with PhotoDeluxe and do make really nice gifts.

To create a monthly or yearly calendar:

1. Click the Calendars button in the Cards & More activity bar.

2. Select Monthly Calendars or Yearly Calendars from the pop-up menu.

   With the exception of selecting a month for monthly calendars, the steps involved in monthly and yearly calendar creation are identical. If you are creating a yearly calendar, skip steps 3 and 4.

3. Click the Month tab and then click the Month button.

4. Select the desired month from the Month dialog box (**Figure 5.4**).

5. Click the Year tab and click on the button that corresponds to the year for which you want to create a calendar.

6. Click the Layout tab and then click the Choose Layout button.

Figure 5.4 The extremely straightforward Month dialog box.

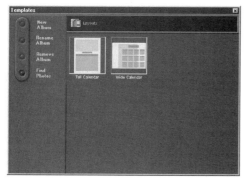

Figure 5.5 The layouts change somewhat in the Templates dialog box depending on whether you are creating a monthly or yearly calendar.

7. In the Templates dialog box (**Figure 5.5**) double-click on the layout that you want to use.

8. Click the Style tab and then click the Choose Style button.

9. Double-click on the style that you want to use.

   As before, all available styles are shown in a Templates palette.

10. Click the Add tab.

11. Use any of the buttons listed in the activity bar to bring an image into PhotoDeluxe.

12. Move and resize the image so that it fits within the calendar opening.

13. Click the Edit tab and read about editing options.

14. Click the Done tab.

CREATING CALENDARS

Creating Single-Page Items

The Pages & Certificates button in the Cards & More activity bar is used to create single-page items such as photo album pages, signs, report covers, certificates, and stationery. All of these items are created using a virtually identical process, which is why they are all presented as one activity. With the exception of selecting a different command to start the process (and choosing from different templates), you will follow the exact same steps: select what you want to create, pick a template to use, and add and position one or more images.

To create a photo album page, sign, report cover, certificate, or stationery:

1. Click the Pages & Certificates button in the Cards & More activity bar.

2. Select the desired command from the pop-up menu.

   Photo Albums provides templates for combining multiple images on a page within artistic borders.

   Signs provides single-image templates with text for garage sales, lost pets, etc.

   Covers provides single-image templates for report or magazine covers.

   Certificates provides full- and partial-page, single-image templates for gift and special event certificates.

   Stationery provides single-image, full-page and envelope templates.

3. Click the Choose Photo Album (or Choose Sign, Choose Cover, etc.) tab.

4. Click the Choose Page (or Choose Sign, Choose Cover, etc.) button.

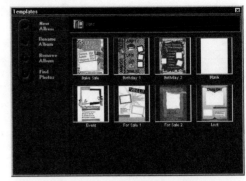

Figure 5.6 Dozens of different border and artwork templates are available from which to choose.

Figure 5.7 All placed images can be moved, resized, or rotated with the sizing and rotation handles.

5. Double-click the template that you want to use in the Templates palette (**Figure 5.6**).

6. Click the Add tab.

7. Use any of the buttons listed in the activity bar to bring an image into PhotoDeluxe.

   See Chapter 3, *Getting Images into PhotoDeluxe* for explanations of each of the different methods available.

8. Move and resize the image so that it fits within the template opening.

   Drag the round rotation handles and solid square handles to rotate or resize the image, or drag the middle of the image to move the image (**Figure 5.7**).

9. Click the Edit tab and read about editing options.

   We recommend editing images separately *before* incorporating them into other activities.

10. Click the Done tab.

Making Labels and Tags

Just as you can use PhotoDeluxe to personalize gifts, you can also use the program to create personalized gift tags, mailing labels, or media labels (for CDs, videotapes, and more).

To create labels or gift tags:

1. Click the Labels & Frames button in the Cards & More activity bar.

2. Select Labels, Media Labels, or Gift Tags from the pop-up menu.

   Labels creates labels of various sizes, for a wide variety of uses.

   Media Labels creates labels for floppy disks, CDs, and videotapes.

   Gift Tags creates colorful tags for Christmas and birthday presents.

3. Click the Choose Label (or Choose Media Label or Choose Gift Tag) tab.

4. Click the Choose Label (or Choose Media Label or Choose Gift Tag) button.

5. From the Templates palette (**Figure 5.8**), double-click the label or tag template that you want to use.

6. Double-click any of the text placeholders to edit the text to suit your needs.

   Double-clicking existing text opens a text-editing dialog box (**Figure 5.9**) within which you can edit and format text.

7. Click the Add tab.

8. Use any of the buttons listed in the activity bar to bring an image into PhotoDeluxe.

9. Move and resize the image so that it fits within the label or tag opening.

10. Click the Edit tab and read about editing options.

11. Click the Done tab.

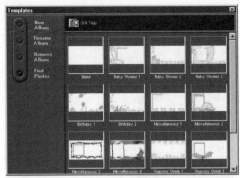

Figure 5.8 The Templates palette contains label or tag artwork within which you can insert a picture.

Figure 5.9 Double-click any placeholder text to edit or format it.

✔ Tip

■ Creating custom labels and tags follows the same basic process we've followed throughout this chapter. One thing to keep in mind, though, is that these items will be relatively small, so you may want to prepare smaller versions of your photos to use with them.

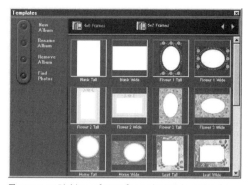

Figure 5.10 Picking a frame for an image is a simple matter of double-clicking on the desired frame.

Framing Images

A simple, but very effective technique you can use is to add artistic frames to your favorite pictures. PhotoDeluxe comes with dozens of different frames. These frames range in style from bold and colorful to elegant and understated. Try them all to find the one that works best for you.

To frame an image:

1. Click the Labels & Frames button in the Cards & More activity bar.

2. Select Frames from the pop-up menu.

3. Click the Choose Frame tab and then click the Choose Frame button.

4. Double-click the frame that you want to use in the Templates palette (**Figure 5.10**). Click any of the three tabs at the top of the Templates palette to view 3 x 5 frames, 4 x 6 frames, or 5 x 7 frames.

5. Click the Add tab.

6. Use any of the buttons listed in the activity bar to bring an image into PhotoDeluxe.

7. Move and resize the image so that it fits within the frame.

8. Click the Edit tab and read about editing options (we feel it is easier to edit the images before using them in other activities), and click the Done tab.

Creating 3D Clip Art

PhotoDeluxe has some simple but fun 3D capabilities, thanks to added functionality from LightWork Design, makers of Kazoo™. There are three 3D activities to choose from: Create 3D Clip Art, View 3D Clip Art, and Create 3D Artwork.

Here we discuss the Create 3D Clip Art activity, which you will probably use most often. The steps you take to complete the Create 3D Artwork activity are very similar, but the concept is a little different. Instead of applying a two-dimensional image to a 3D object, you insert a 3D object into a 2D image. The View 3D Clip Art activity simply launches the Kazoo 3D viewer so you can view and play with existing Kazoo 3D files.

To create 3D clip art:

1. Click the 3D Activities button in the Cards and More activity bar.

2. From the resulting pop-up menu choose the Create 3D Clip Art command (**Figure 5.11**).

3. Click the Instructions tab and read the basic instructions for this activity.

4. Click the Add Background tab.

5. Use any of the buttons shown in the activity bar (**Figure 5.12**) to open the image you want to use as your *background* image.
   Chapter 3, *Getting Images into PhotoDeluxe* discusses all of these buttons.

6. Click the Add Photo tab.

7. Use any of the buttons shown in the activity bar to open the image you want to *add to the 3D object* itself.

Figure 5.11 In addition to creating 3D clip art, you can also view 3D clip art and add 3D objects to other images.

Figure 5.12 Open images for a 3D activity using these familiar activities.

Figure 5.13 3D models are stored in an album, just like any other image, making them easy to select and open.

Figure 5.14 After all image and 3D objects are selected, they are composited together in this Kazoo 3D window.

8. Click the Album tab.

9. Click the Open Album button.

10. From the 3D Models album window that appears (**Figure 5.13**), double-click the 3D model that you want to use.

    This brings up the Kazoo 3D window (**Figure 5.14**).

11. Within the Kazoo 3D window click the Rotate, Roll, Move, or Zoom buttons in the upper-left corner of the window, then press and drag within the window to rotate, roll, move, or zoom the 3D object.

12. When you are satisfied with the position and orientation of the 3D object, click the OK button to save the Kazoo file.

13. In the Save Kazoo file dialog box that appears, name the file and click the Save button.

    This returns you to the Create 3D Clip Art activity.

14. Click the Done tab to exit the Create 3D Clip Art activity.

CREATING 3D CLIP ART

Creating PhotoParades

If you are looking for a fun and impressive way to share your photos with others, a PhotoParade just might be the answer. A PhotoParade is a collection of images that appears within an animated slideshow, complete with transition effects and opening and closing graphics. The primary disadvantages of a PhotoParade are the relatively large size of the PhotoParade file and the cartoon nature of the PhotoParade themes. While you can play a PhotoParade without a theme (called a Carousel in PhotoParade-lingo), there is no way during the creation of the PhotoParade to select Carousel as the default viewing method.

To create a PhotoParade:

1. Click the PhotoParade button in the Cards & More activity bar.

2. Select Create a PhotoParade from the pop-up menu.

3. Click the Album tab.

   Because PhotoParades are created from open images, all currently open images will be closed when you click the Album tab.

4. Click the Open Album button.

   The My Photos window opens.

5. Click the Photos tab in the activity bar.

6. Click the Add Photo button.

7. Navigate through the Open dialog box to locate and open the first file that you want added to the PhotoParade.

8. Continue adding photos until you have added all photos that you want in the PhotoParade.

   To remove a photo, select it in the PhotoParade gallery and click the Remove Photo button.

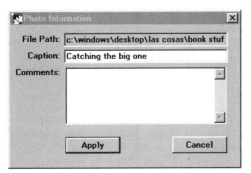

Figure 5.15 Use this dialog box to title and caption your photos.

Figure 5.16 These themes are your only choices when creating a PhotoParade.

9. Click the Captions tab.

10. Select a photo in the PhotoParade gallery and click the Add Caption button.

11. In the Edit Photo Information dialog box (**Figure 5.15**), edit the title and caption as desired, then click the Close button.

    You can also use the Next and Previous buttons to add captions to all images without leaving the dialog box.

12. Click the Theme tab.

13. Select a theme from the Choose Theme drop-down list (**Figure 5.16**).

14. Click the Build tab.

15. Select a segment size from the Segment Size drop-down list.

    Unsegmented creates a single PhotoParade file. This is a good choice for PhotoParades that will stay on your hard drive or will be sent on a Zip disk or other high-capacity media.

    1 MB, 1.4 MB (Floppy), and 2 MB (AOL) create segments of 1, 1.4 and 2 MBs for transfer over the Internet, via floppy disk, or over AOL. (Many Internet service providers limit e-mail attachments to 1 MB. AOL limits attachments to 2 MB.)

16. Click the Build PhotoParade button.

17. Name the PhotoParade file in the PhotoParade dialog box and click the Save button.

18. Click the OK button at the confirmation dialog box, which appears once the PhotoParade file has been built.

19. Click the Play tab and the Play PhotoParade button if you want to see what the PhotoParade looks like.

20. Click the Done tab.

CREATING PHOTOPARADES

To play a PhotoParade:

1. Click the PhotoParade button in the Cards & More activity bar.

2. Select Play a PhotoParade from the pop-up menu.

3. Use the Choose a PhotoParade to Play dialog box to locate and open the PhotoParade that you want to view.

4. The selected PhotoParade begins automatically (**Figure 5.17**).

5. At the PhotoParade information screen (**Figure 5.18**) that appears after the PhotoParade finishes, click the Quit PhotoParade button and then click the Exit button to return to PhotoDeluxe.

✔ Tip

■ Titles and captions do not appear when viewing images in the standard PhotoParade mode. To see this information, you will have to escape out of the PhotoParade once it starts playing, switch to the Carousel mode, and then restart the PhotoParade. If you are sending your PhotoParade to someone else and you want them to see the titles and captions, you will have to send them instructions on how to switch the PhotoParade to Carousel mode.

Figure 5.17 A PhotoParade in action.

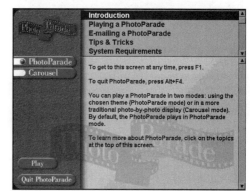

Figure 5.18 This screen contains useful information about working with PhotoParades.

6

SHARING

PhotoDeluxe's Share activity bar makes it easy to share photos with family and friends all over the world. The Share activity bar has two main modes, Web sharing and seasonal sharing, each of which contains buttons for specific activities or destinations.

Web sharing is the default mode (but it can also be activated, if necessary, by clicking the Web Sharing button). The activities in the Web sharing mode are static and include activities for sending images via e-mail, creating Web-based projects, and sharing a collection of images on the Web via Adobe eCircles, which is a Web-based method of storing and sharing images and image projects. There are also buttons for simply connecting to the Adobe eCircles Web site for information or to sign up for an account.

The Seasonal Sharing button activates the second set of activities, for creating seasonal or holiday cards, tags, and more. From time to time when you start PhotoDeluxe, you will be prompted to download additional seasonal activities, depending on the time of year. Follow the on-screen prompts to connect to the Internet and download additional available activities. Once downloaded, these new guided activities can be used like any others.

Sending Images with E-mail

One of the easiest ways to share images with friends and family is to simply send them an e-mail message and attach the image to that message. This process is both fast and simple, and can be accomplished without ever leaving PhotoDeluxe.

Note: To send e-mail messages from within PhotoDeluxe you must have a properly configured e-mail account (usually provided by your Internet service provider) and an available Internet connection.

Figure 6.1 The Email button makes it easy to send an image to someone without ever leaving PhotoDeluxe.

To send an image via e-mail:

1. Click the Share button in the upper-left corner, above the Open Photo listing.

2. Click the Email button in the Activity Bar (**Figure 6.1**).

3. In the Email Information dialog box (**Figure 6.2**), in the Send To line, type the e-mail address of the person to whom you want to send the image.

4. Type your e-mail address in the From line.

5. Type a subject in the Subject line.

6. Type your message in the Message area.

7. Click the Attach File button.

Figure 6.2 All information in this dialog box must be completed before you can send the message.

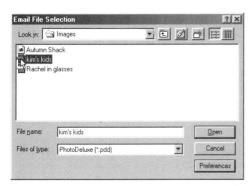

Figure 6.3 Use this standard dialog box to select and attach the image you want to send.

8. In the Email File Selection dialog box (**Figure 6.3**), locate and select the file that you want to send.

   By default, this dialog box only lists PhotoDeluxe (*.pdd) files, but you can use the Files of type drop-down list to make other types of files visible as well.

9. Click the Open button to exit this dialog box and attach the file to your e-mail message.

10. Click the Send button in the Email Information dialog box to send the e-mail message and the attached image.

SENDING IMAGES WITH E-MAIL

Creating a Web-based Postcard or Puzzle

Figure 6.4 PhotoDeluxe offers these two Web-based projects.

PhotoDeluxe works in partnership on some of the Share guided activities with Adobe eCircles, a service for maintaining a collection of images on the Web, rather than on your own computer. By maintaining these images on the Web, friends, family, and colleagues can access the images for viewing or printing at any time. This is a huge advantage over having to e-mail the images to everyone you want to share them with.

In order to complete this activity, you will need to follow the Adobe eCircles onscreen prompts to either sign up for an eCircles account or to log into an existing account. The eCircles service is free of charge, though, so don't hesitate to take advantage of it.

Because the Adobe eCircles service is Web-based and subject to change at any time, the specific steps within Adobe eCircles are not listed individually. However, you can follow the very simple on-screen prompts to complete this activity.

Note: You must have an image open *before* starting this activity. Unlike most activities, there is no way to open an image once you have begun, and you cannot continue past the first step in the activity without an image open.

To create a Web postcard or puzzle:

1. Click the Share button in the upper-left corner, above the Open Photo listing.

2. Click the Web Project button in the Share activity bar (make sure this activity bar is in the Web Sharing mode).

3. Click the Choose tab to start the activity.

Figure 6.5 This e-mail information lets Adobe eCircles notify the recipient that you have posted an image for them to view.

Figure 6.6 Any button but Cancel takes you to the Adobe eCircles Web site.

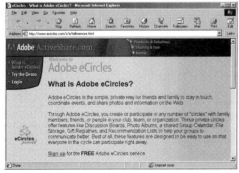

Figure 6.7 eCircles is an Internet company that has partnered with Adobe to provide a way for people to share images over the Internet.

4. Click the Picture Postcard or Picture Puzzle button (**Figure 6.4**) to select the type of activity you want.
Picture Postcard is the default selection.

5. Click the Email tab.

6. Click the Email button.

7. Fill in the Email Information dialog box with the recipient's e-mail address, your e-mail address, a caption for your image, and any message that you want to include (**Figure 6.5**).

8. Click the OK button to exit this dialog box.

9. Click the Post tab.

10. Click the Post to Web button.
This will start your default Internet connection and bring up the Share on Web informational dialog box (**Figure 6.6**).

11. Follow the on-screen prompts in the Share on Web dialog box to learn more about Adobe eCircles (**Figure 6.7**), sign up for Adobe eCircles, access your existing Adobe eCircles account, and post your project.

12. If necessary, exit your Web browser when finished to return to PhotoDeluxe.

13. Click the Done tab.

Sharing Photos on the Web

Even without creating special projects, you can use Adobe eCircles to share images with friends and family on the Web. This guided activity is similar to the Web Projects activity above, but can be used to share a collection of images, rather than a project made from a single image. Images are selected from existing albums, so you must already have the desired images saved in albums (See Chapter 7, *Saving and Exporting Images*).

Like the Web Projects activity, this activity uses Adobe eCircles as the destination for your images, so you will need to create or log onto your eCircles account to complete the final steps in the activity.

To share a photo on the Web:

1. Click the Share button in the upper-left corner, above the Open Photo listing.

2. Click the Share on Web button in the Share activity bar.

   Make sure this activity bar is in the Web Sharing mode (click the Web Sharing button, if necessary).

3. Click the Open Web Album tab to start the activity.

4. Click the Web Album button.

   This opens the Post to Web album window (**Figure 6.8**).

5. Click the Get Photos tab.

   This tab lists all of the ways you can get an image into PhotoDeluxe (**Figure 6.9**), but it's very misleading. To complete this activity, you must move images into the Post to Web album, which can only be done by dragging them there from *another* album. Therefore, the Open File, Cameras, Scanners, and Other buttons

Figure 6.8 Only the images within this album will be posted to the Web.

Figure 6.9 Of these methods for bringing an image into PhotoDeluxe, only the My Photos, Sample Photos, Clip Art, and Changeables buttons bring up the necessary album windows.

Figure 6.10 The only way to get images into the Post to Web album is to drag them there from another album.

are not helpful for this activity, even though they can be used here to open an image.

6. Click the My Photos, Sample Photos, Clip Art, or Changeables button to open one of these album organizer windows.

7. Drag one or more images from another album into the Post to Web album window (**Figure 6.10**).

8. Close all album windows except for the Post to Web album.

9. Click the Post tab in the activity bar.

10. Click the Post to Web button.
This will start your default Internet connection and bring up the Share on Web informational dialog box.

11. Follow the on-screen prompts to learn more about Adobe eCircles, sign up for Adobe eCircles, access your existing Adobe eCircles account, and post your images.

12. If necessary, exit your Web browser when finished to return to PhotoDeluxe.

13. Click the Done tab.

Creating Holiday Cards, Tags, and More

One great use for PhotoDeluxe that is literally "fun for the whole family" is to create and send customized holiday cards, add personalized gift tags to presents, create trading cards, and much more. Each button in the Seasonal Sharing section of the Share activity bar corresponds to a different holiday, season or theme, and the pop-up menus for each of these buttons list a wide variety of activities. Using these activities, you can have fun creating these cards (and more) and your family and friends can be amazed and amused when they receive them.

To create a holiday greeting card or other project:

1. In the Share activity bar, click the Seasonal Sharing button.

2. Locate and click the button that corresponds to the holiday you want to use.

3. Select the desired project from the resulting pop-up menu (such as Frames, Labels, Photo Album, or Greeting Cards) (**Figure 6.11**).

   An appropriate background graphic will open.

4. Click the View tab at the top of the activity bar.

5. Click the Front, Back, or Inside button in the image window to locate the opening for your photo (**Figure 6.12**).

6. Click the Add tab.

7. Open the images that you want to add to the calendar using any of the buttons in the activity bar.

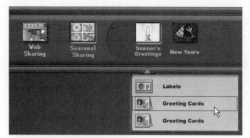

Figure 6.11 Most major holidays have activities to create cards.

Figure 6.12 Holiday cards have three different views: Front, Back, and Inside.

Figure 6.13 This happy couple is now the centerpiece of a unique Christmas card for friends and family.

Figure 6.14 As holidays approach, you will be prompted to install new seasonal sharing activities.

8. Move and resize the photos or other images until you are happy with their position on the background graphic (**Figure 6.13**).

9. Click the Edit tab if you need to fix or apply special effects to any of your photos.

10. Click the Done tab.

✔ Tip

■ Don't worry if there are no activities listed for seasonal sharing. As new holidays or seasons approach you will be prompted to install new activities from the PhotoDeluxe CD (**Figure 6.14**).

PART 3

OUTPUT

Output

PhotoDeluxe offers two different options for what you can do with your images once you have finished working with them: printing and exporting. Printing is pretty much what you would expect (transferring digital images onto paper or some other surface), but PhotoDeluxe provides some interesting and useful options regarding how your images print. You can print them on paper or any other media (even t-shirt transfers), print several copies of an image on a page or several different images on a page, and much more.

Exporting PhotoDeluxe images is what lets you use your images in other programs, such as Photoshop or PageMaker, or prepare them for use on the Web. PhotoDeluxe supports a wide variety of file formats so you should be able to take your images into just about any application in any operating system.

SAVING AND EXPORTING IMAGES

7

Unless you have been using your computer for less than an hour, you are probably well aware of the importance of saving your work periodically. This is especially true in a graphics application like PhotoDeluxe, in which you will undoubtedly be doing a lot of "experimenting."

In addition to simply saving your work, PhotoDeluxe offers a wide range of export options, from simply exporting an image to a different file format to creating "slide show" screen savers for Windows.

Saving an Image to Disk

No matter what file format an image is in when it comes into PhotoDeluxe, you will need to save it in PhotoDeluxe format if you want to be able to do simple saves (using [Ctrl]-[S], for example) as you work. PhotoDeluxe offers a very brief guided activity to create a PhotoDeluxe version of your image.

To save an image:

1. Click the Save & Send button in the Get & Fix Photo activity bar.

2. Choose the Save command from the pop-up menu.

   You can also simply use the Save and Save As commands from the File menu, which work as they do in any Windows application (with the addition of the album feature).

3. In the resulting Save As dialog box (**Figure 7.1**), enter a name for the file.

4. Specify the folder or disk location into which you want the file to be saved.

5. For easier access to this image, use the Add to Album pop-up list to select a PhotoDeluxe album to place a thumbnail of the image into.

   If you do not want to add this image to an album, deselect the "Add to Album" checkbox and skip the next step.

6. In the Title field, replace the "Untitled-1" text with a name for the album thumbnail.

7. Click the Save button.

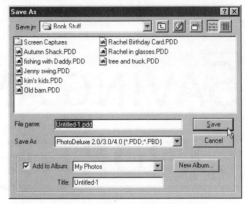

Figure 7.1 A standard Save As dialog box with PhotoDeluxe Album options.

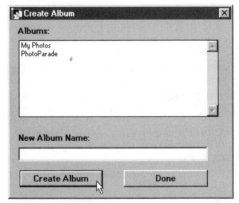

Figure 7.2 Create as many new albums as you need to help you organize your images.

✔ Tip

- To help you organize your images, you can create as many albums as you want. Simply click the New Album button in the Save As dialog box, enter a name for your new album in the Create Album dialog box (**Figure 7.2**), and click the Create Album button. Make as many new albums as you want, and then click the Done button to return to the Save As dialog box. These new albums appear in the "Add to Album" pop-up list.

SAVING AN IMAGE TO DISK

File Format Babylon

There are dozens of different file formats in the world of computer graphics, but you will probably only ever need to use two or three of them. Here are brief explanations of the export file formats that PhotoDeluxe supports, listed in the order in which you will most likely encounter them.

JPEG is the standard file format for photographic images that are displayed or transferred over the Internet. JPEG stands for *Joint Photographic Experts Group*. JPEG is a *lossy* compression scheme (that is, some data is lost each time you compress the file), so always edit the original, uncompressed file and then save it again (as a JPEG). Recompressing an already-compressed JPEG file will degrade the quality of the image.

GIF (*Graphics Interchange Format*) is the most common file format (along with JPEG) for Web images. Unlike JPEG, GIF works best for images that contain large areas of similar color (illustrations rather than photographs). Technically, GIF is supposed to be pronounced "jif," but as far as we're concerned, "Jif " is a peanut butter (and a darn good one, too). Most of the people we know pronounce GIF with a hard "g," as in "graphics," the word it represents. GIF is also a lossy compression scheme.

BMP (a compression of the word *bitmap*) is the standard Windows file format for pixel-based images (that is, those made up of a bunch of tiny dots). BMP is the format used for all PhotoDeluxe grayscale images.

EPS stands for *Encapsulated PostScript*, and is the industry-standard format for illustration programs and high-end printers. Use this format for files that will be imported into page-layout programs or sent to professional print shops or service bureaus.

PICT (short for *pict*ure) files are very rarely encountered outside of the Macintosh operating system. On the Macintosh, PICT files are frequently used in illustration and page layout programs.

PNG is the latest in a long line of alphabet soup file formats for the Web. PNG stands for *Portable Network Graphics*, and is similar to GIF, but with no loss of image quality and better support for transparency. Unfortunately, not all Web browsers support the PNG format yet, although this won't be the case for long.

Indexed-color files contain a maximum of 256 colors. Since many older computers cannot display more than 256 colors, the indexed-color format is used when you want to ensure that all computers will be able to display the image properly (when viewed on a Web page, for example). However, since the GIF format also creates an indexed-color file, and includes file compression, it is used far more often than indexed-color alone.

Photoshop format creates a file that can be opened and manipulated in Adobe Photoshop, a high-end and extraordinarily capable image-editing program. Specifically, the Photoshop file format preserves PhotoDeluxe layers (except for text layers, which are converted to uneditable bitmaps).

Acrobat format is used to create a platform- and software-independent, compressed file that can be read by any computer using the Macintosh, Windows, UNIX, or DOS operating systems, as long as they have the (free) Acrobat Reader software.

FlashPix is a file format developed by Kodak to facilitate the transfer and display of large, high-resolution files. Needless to say, this is a good idea, but it only works in applications that specifically support the FlashPix format, and not all do.

Exporting to a Different File Format

One of the disadvantages of doing your image editing in PhotoDeluxe is that it forces you to use its own proprietary file format while you work. In order to use your images in other applications, you will need to export the images into a file format that other applications can work with.

Do this as the last step, after you have made any changes to your image in PhotoDeluxe. If you make additional changes after exporting the file, you will need to export it again.

To export an image:

1. Click the Save & Send button in the Get & Fix Photo activity bar.

2. Choose Export from the pop-up menu.

3. Click the Export tab.

4. Click on the file format that you want to use.

    The Export dialog box appears for all formats except GIF Format or Index Color, which have additional options.

    See the "File Format Babylon" sidebar for a discussion of the pros and cons of each format.

5. If you chose GIF Format or Index Color, click the OK button in the Options dialog box (**Figure 7.3**).

    PhotoDeluxe converts your image according to the format you selected in step 4.

6. In the Export dialog box (**Figure 7.4**), enter a name for the file and click the Save button.

    You can add files to an album from this dialog box in the same fashion as you would from a standard Save As dialog box.

7. Click the Done tab.

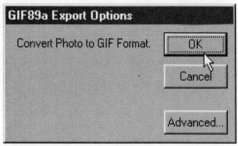

Figure 7.3 Click OK in this dialog box for the recommended file format options.

Figure 7.4 The Export dialog box.

✔ Tip

■ Instead of selecting from just the four different file formats that have their own buttons, we generally just use the Other Export button in the Export tab. This takes you directly to the Export dialog box, where you can select from a list of all of the export file formats that PhotoDeluxe supports. You can then select the format you need, including some of the lesser known formats like PNG or FlashPix.

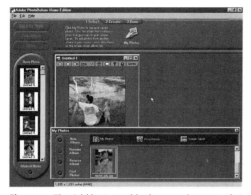

Figure 7.5 The Add button adds the open image to the Screen Saver album.

Creating a Screen Saver

One slick trick that you can do to impress your friends and family is to create a Windows screen saver to display a bunch of images on your computer monitor. This is also a nice way to present a "slide show" of images without having to use a separate application. You can only have one of these screen savers at a time, but it is easy to add or remove images from it.

To create a screen saver:

1. Click the Save & Send button in the Get & Fix Photo activity bar.

2. Choose Screen Saver from the pop-up menu.

3. Click the Select tab.

4. Click the My Photos button.

5. Click the button at the top of the My Photos palette to select the album that contains the photos that you want to include in your screen saver.

6. Drag the thumbnail of the image you want to use on to the Screen Saver album button at the top of the My Photos palette to add the image to the Screen Saver album (**Figure 7.5**).

7. Repeat steps 5 and 6 to add additional images to the Screen Saver album.

8. Click the Create tab.

(continues on next page)

CREATING A SCREEN SAVER

9. Click the Create button.

This creates a PhotoDeluxe screen saver and sets it as the active screen saver for Windows. To preview this screen saver or to select a different screen saver, right-click on the Windows desktop, choose Properties from the shortcut menu, and then click the Screen Saver tab in the Display Properties dialog box (**Figure 7.6**).

10. Click the Done tab.

✔ Tip

■ You do not have to use the Screen Saver activity to add or remove images from the Screen Saver album. You can add images to the album as you would to any album during a normal save or export. You can remove images from the album by right-clicking on the image thumbnail in the album and choosing the Remove command. However, to update the screen saver for Windows, you do need to run the Screen Saver guided activity, click the Create tab, and click the Create button.

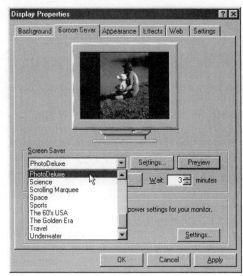

Figure 7.6 The PhotoDeluxe Slide Show is now available in the list of Windows screen savers.

Figure 7.7 This fall scene makes for an interesting desktop image.

Creating Windows Wallpaper

If you've ever envied a friend or coworker who had a cool desktop image on his or her computer, PhotoDeluxe has a guided activity just for you. In six easy steps you can turn any image into a full-screen desktop image (**Figure 7.7**) which you can not only use on your computer, but can easily share with others (that is, if you feel like sharing).

Note: This process works best on an image that is the same size as your desktop (typically 640 by 480 pixels or 800 by 600 pixels). If your image is smaller, it will not fill the screen. If your image is bigger, the outer portions of the image will not display.

To create wallpaper:

1. Open the image that you want to use as wallpaper.

2. Click the Save & Send button in the Get & Fix Photo activity bar.

3. Choose Windows Wallpaper from the pop-up menu.

4. Click the Wallpaper tab.

5. Click the Wallpaper button.

   This creates a .bmp file in the C:\Windows directory which can now be selected as wallpaper in the Display Properties dialog box. Right-click on the Windows desktop and select Properties from the shortcut menu to access this dialog box.

6. Click the Done tab.

Transferring an Image to Adobe PageMill

Adobe PageMill is a popular Web page-creation software. Because both PageMill and PhotoDeluxe are Adobe products, it should come as no surprise that it is very easy to transfer images from PhotoDeluxe to PageMill.

This process is great if you use PageMill, but even if you don't you can still use this process to get your PhotoDeluxe images into whatever application you are using to create your Web pages. If you cannot drag the final image directly into your Web authoring application, you can always just export the file, as discussed earlier in this chapter.

To transfer an image to PageMill:

1. Open the image that you want to transfer to Adobe PageMill.

2. Click the Save & Send button in the Get & Fix Photo activity bar.

3. Choose PageMill from the pop-up menu.

4. Click the Trim tab and trim the image to the desired size, if necessary.

   See "Rotating, Flipping, and Trimming Images" in Chapter 4, *Modifying Images*, for more information on trimming.

5. Click the Size tab.

6. If necessary, resize the image by clicking the Photo Size button and entering the desired image size in the Photo Size dialog box (**Figure 7.8**).

7. Click the Reduce tab.

8. Click the Reduce Resolution button to reduce the image resolution to 72 dpi.

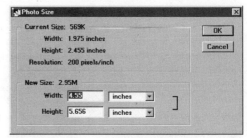

Figure 7.8 Enter new height and width values in this dialog box to resize your image precisely.

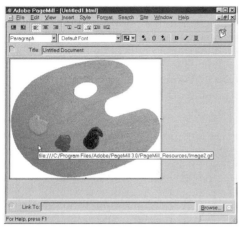

Figure 7.9 Drag the image from PhotoDeluxe to the PageMill taskbar button, and then into PageMill itself.

9. Click the Drag & Drop tab.

10. Click the Select All button.

11. Drag the image down out of the PhotoDeluxe window and onto the Taskbar button for Adobe PageMill. Keep the mouse button held down until the PageMill window opens, then move the cursor up into the PageMill application window (**Figure 7.9**) and release the mouse button.

12. Switch to the PhotoDeluxe application window and click the Done tab.

PRINTING IMAGES

Before we got a nice color printer, we spent a lot of time *describing* to friends and family how great our photos looked after having been scanned and retouched. Now we can actually *show* them how great the photos look.

There are many color printers out there and almost all of the name-brand ones (HP, Canon, Apple) provide good output. If you want to do a lot of photographic work, however, make sure you look at samples before you buy. It's even a good idea to take in an image on a floppy disk and have the salesperson print it out on a couple of different printers before you shell out the $250 to $400. Keep in mind also that while color printers are less expensive than laser printers, the per-page cost of printing is much higher. We recommend using a laser printer for proofs, and a color printer for final images or for color proofs only. That is, of course, only if you already have a laser printer. We don't recommend buying one just for proofs.

Setting up the Page

Before printing for the first time, it is a good idea to change (or at least check) your page setup. This is also important if you switch back and forth between two or more printers. For example, if you use a laser printer or inexpensive color printer for quick image proofs, and then switch to a nice color printer for final printouts, be sure to check your page setup before the final printouts on the more expensive color printer.

To change page setup:

1. Click the Print button on the Get & Fix Photo activity bar.

2. Select Page Setup from the pop-up menu.

3. From the Name list in the Printer section of the Page Setup dialog box (**Figure 8.1**), select the printer that you want to use.

4. From the Size and Source lists in the Paper section, select the paper size and paper source (a paper tray or manual feed).

5. Select Portrait (taller than wide) or Landscape (wider than tall) orientation.

6. To set options for your printer, click the Properties button, set any desired printer-specific options, and click the OK button to return to the Page Setup dialog box.

7. Click the OK button to exit the Page Setup dialog box and return to PhotoDeluxe. You are now ready to print.

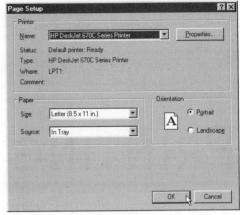

Figure 8.1 The Page Setup dialog box.

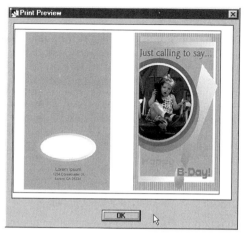

Figure 8.2 The Print Preview dialog box.

Previewing Images

For images that combine many different elements, such as photo composites, greeting cards, and calendars, you can get a better idea of how the finished product will look by using a print preview, rather than simply viewing the image in the work window. The Print Preview command opens a dialog box with a small but otherwise accurate rendition of what your image will look like on paper.

To preview an image:

1. Click the Print button in the Get & Fix Photo activity bar.

2. Select Print Preview from the pop-up menu.

   Your image is displayed in a Print Preview dialog box (**Figure 8.2**).

3. Click the OK button to exit the print preview.

Printing Single Images

Printing images is accomplished with the Print Standard Sizes command, which lets you print one or more copies of the same image on a page. (This command also lets you add different photos to a page, as discussed in the next section, "Printing Multiple Images.") By following the Print Standard Sizes guided activity, you select the style and layout you want to use, and then print the image.

To print an image:

1. Click the Print button in the Get & Fix Photo activity bar.

2. Select Print Standard Sizes from the pop-up menu.

3. Click the Style tab, and click the Single Photo Repeated button.

   This option is used even for a single instance of a photo.

4. Click the Layout tab, and click the Choose Layout button.

5. In the Choose Paper Type dialog box (**Figure 8.3**), select the type of paper you want to print on from the mislabeled "Select the Brand of Paper" menu.

   Avery lets you choose from different Avery label and paper sizes (**Figure 8.4**).

   Plain Paper gives you no choice but to print to whatever paper is loaded in your printer.

   Standard Photo Print Size lets you select from standard photo print sizes.

6. Click the Add tab.

   This tab is not used for single images, but gives you the option to preview the image, if desired, by clicking the Preview button.

7. Click the Print tab to print the image.

8. Click the Done tab to exit this activity.

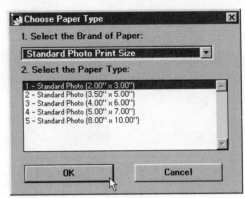

Figure 8.3 Choose the type of paper you will print on from this dialog box.

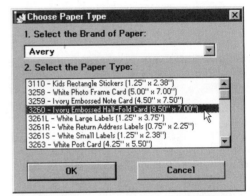

Figure 8.4 PhotoDeluxe supports a wide variety of Avery labels and paper types.

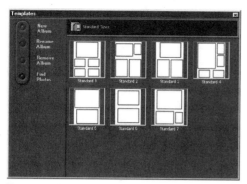

Figure 8.5 Choose a multiple-image template from this dialog box.

Figure 8.6 Drag the images in the Open Photos list (at the left) onto the image placeholders in the template.

Printing Multiple Images

In addition to printing single images, PhotoDeluxe also lets you print several different images on the same page. While you could do this by combining photographs or clip art into one image, it is often faster and more convenient to simply combine separate images for printing.

To print multiple images on a page:

1. Open all images that you want to print.

2. Click the Print button in the Get & Fix Photo activity bar.

3. Select Print Standard Sizes from the pop-up menu.

4. Click the Style tab.

5. Click the Different Photos button.

   All open images are removed from the work window. They are not closed, however, and are still available from the Open Photos list at the left side of the PhotoDeluxe interface.

6. Click the Layout tab.

7. Click the Choose Layout button.

8. In the Templates dialog box (**Figure 8.5**), double-click the type of layout you want to use. This opens a blank template in the work area.

9. Click the Add tab.

10. Drag the images that you want to print from the Open Photos list to the desired placeholders in the template window (**Figure 8.6**).

    If you want to use an image that is not already open, you can open it using any of the buttons in the activity bar.

11. Click the Print tab to print the image.

12. Click the Done tab to exit this activity.

PRINTING MULTIPLE IMAGES

Printing Multiple Copies of an Image on a Page

For stickers, labels, or wallet-sized photos, printing a whole sheet of images is the most efficient way to go. PhotoDeluxe lets you choose from a wide variety of formats, including Avery labels and paper products, and standard paper sizes.

To print multiple copies of an image on a page:

1. Open the image that you want to print.

2. Click the Print button in the Get & Fix Photo activity bar.

3. Select Print Multiple on a Page from the pop-up menu.

4. In the Print Multiple dialog box (**Figure 8.7**), select the number of copies that you want printed across the page and down the page.

   PhotoDeluxe does not resize the images to fit the page, so you are limited to the maximum number of images that fit as is across and down the page.

5. If you don't like the way the images are distributed across the page, click the Change button and select a different paper type or size, or select from a list of Avery labels and papers (**Figure 8.8**). Click the OK button in the Choose Paper Type dialog box to return to the Print Multiple dialog box.

6. Click the Print button.

7. In the Print dialog box (**Figure 8.9**), set your preferred print options (print quality, number of copies, etc.), and click the OK button.

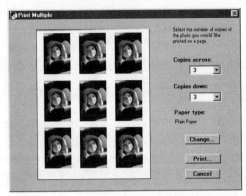

Figure 8.7 This dialog box lets you set the number of copies of an image that appear on a printed page.

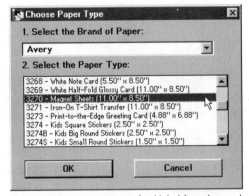

Figure 8.8 These paper types (and labels) can be used to print multiple copies of the same image on a page.

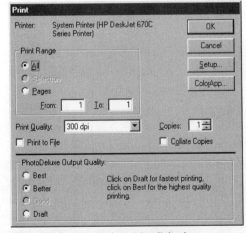

Figure 8.9 The PhotoDeluxe Print dialog box.

Printing T-shirt Transfers

The perfect gift for any proud parent or grandparent is a t-shirt that bears the face of a loved one. Creating t-shirt transfers is almost as easy as simply printing the image. The part that we don't care for is having to do more ironing, which is the only way to get the image from the transfer sheet onto the t-shirt itself.

To print a T-shirt transfer:

1. Open the image that you want to print.

2. Click the Print button in the Get & Fix Photo activity bar.

3. Select Print T-Shirt Transfer from the pop-up menu.

4. Click the T-Shirt tab.

5. Click the T-Shirt button.

6. The Print dialog box appears.

7. Load a transfer sheet into your printer and click the OK button in the Print dialog box. This produces a mirror image of your photo or image that you can then iron onto a t-shirt.

8. Click the Done tab.

PRINTING T-SHIRT TRANSFERS

Adjusting Color Printing

Ensuring color consistency between what
you see on your computer monitor and what
you get from your printer can be a frustrating
experience. PhotoDeluxe makes the process
relatively painless with the Adjust Color
Printing dialog box. Essentially, you just tell
PhotoDeluxe the kind of printer you are using,
then compare a sheet of thumbnail images to
the original and pick the best match. What
this lacks in precise control is, we feel, more
than made up for in speed and simplicity.

To adjust an image for color printing:

1. Click the Print button in the Get & Fix
   Photo activity bar.

2. Select Adjust Color Printing from the
   pop-up menu.

3. Select the "Adjust color printing" option
   in the Adjust Color Printing dialog box
   (**Figure 8.10**).

4. Select your printer type from the list of
   supported printers (**Figure 8.11**).

5. Click the More button.

6. Click the Print button to print thumbnails of the sample image.

7. Compare the printout of the thumbnails
   to the sample image, and in the dialog
   box click the numbered button that corresponds to the thumbnail location that
   most closely matches the sample image
   (**Figure 8.12**).

8. Click the OK button.

   Based on your choice of thumbnails,
   PhotoDeluxe will adjust the image information that it sends to your printer to
   produce printed images that more accu-
   rately reflect on-screen colors.

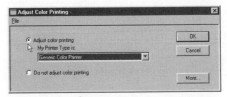

Figure 8.10 The simple version of the Adjust Color
Printing dialog box.

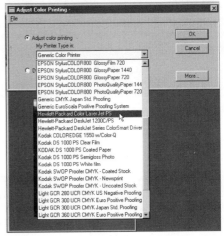

Figure 8.11 Virtually all consumer-level color
printers are included in this list.

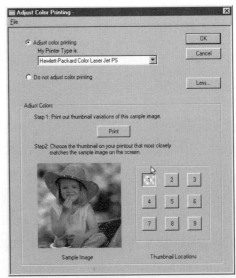

Figure 8.12 Easy color calibration is accomplished by
clicking the button for the printed version that best
matches the sample image.

PART 4

ADVANCED TECHNIQUES

Advanced Techniques

In the chapters you've read up to this point, you've only seen half of what PhotoDeluxe is capable of doing. To be more accurate, you've used most of PhotoDeluxe's features, but you haven't learned how to implement those features to their full potential. For example, you've learned how to follow a guided activity to place two images in the same file, but not how to create your own collages using elements from a dozen or more images. You've learned how to make a rectangular selection around an object, but not how to use several different selection tools to create a precise selection around a complex image element. You've learned how to paint on an image with a color, but not how to combine different painting layers to create amazing effects that are simply impossible with a single color, or even multiple colors on a single layer. This next section will show you how to do all of these things, and much more.

In addition, you will work with a wide variety of the special effects filters that come with PhotoDeluxe, use some no-nonsense techniques for correcting common image problems, and learn how to use PhotoDeluxe to prepare images for use on the Web or for sending to another person via an e-mail message.

SELECTION
TECHNIQUES

One of the key skills you will need to develop to perform any of the more advanced tasks in PhotoDeluxe is that of selecting image areas or elements. If you want to insert yourself (or anyone else) behind the podium on awards night, or replace a dull gray sky with a beautiful blue one, or apply a special effect to just part of an image, you'll have to master selecting first. And, as luck would have it, that's just what you'll do in this chapter.

Note: To make the selections easier to see, the backgrounds have been removed from many of the illustrative graphics in this chapter. See Chapter 10, *Combining Images*, for information on isolating image elements.

Understanding the Selection Tools

PhotoDeluxe provides nine separate tools for selecting images or portions of images. The Object selection tool is used to select and manipulate entire image objects; the Polygon and Trace tools are used to select freeform areas of an image; the Rectangle, Oval, Square, and Circle selection tools are used to select shaped parts of an image; the Color Wand is used to select areas of similar color; and the SmartSelect tool is used to trace an image area based on color borders within the image. Each of these nine tools is discussed separately in the following pages, but all of the tools except the Object selection tool and the SmartSelect tool share common functionality, and all of the selection tools are accessed from either the Select menu (**Figure 9.1**) or the Selections palette (**Figure 9.2**).

For all of the selection tools except for the Object selection tool and the SmartSelect tool, the Selections palette will contain seven buttons, in addition to the drop-down list of tools. These buttons are labeled and used as follows:

New is used to create a new selection. Previously selected areas of the image will become deselected.

Add creates a new selection, but leaves the previous selection intact. This allows you to select two or more separate areas, or to combine shapes for interesting selections (**Figure 9.3**).

Reduce removes the selected area from the previous selection, allowing you to create selection "cut-outs."

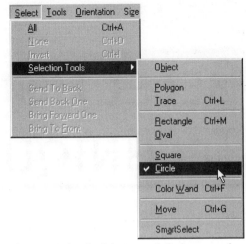

Figure 9.1 Using the Select menu is the long way of choosing a selection tool.

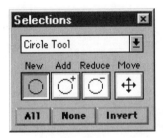

Figure 9.2 With the Selections palette, all of the selection tools (and variations) are immediately available.

Figure 9.3 Adding two circular selections lets us isolate the faces of these two girls.

Move switches you to the Object selection tool so that you can drag the selected part of the image to a new location.

All, **None**, and **Invert**, are fairly self-explanatory, selecting everything, nothing, or the opposite of what is currently selected.

✔ Tips

- Instead of clicking the Move button to move the selected part of the image, you can simply press and drag from inside any selection to move the selected image area as long as the New button is active. This avoids the annoyance of having to change selection tools every time you want to move something.

- As you work with selections, you will make a lot of mistakes, creating unwanted selections or unwittingly altering existing selections. While you can use the Undo command to correct your most recent mistake, the easiest way to deal with multiple mistakes is often to simply remove the selection and start over again. And the quickest way to do this is with the keyboard equivalent for clicking the None button, (Ctrl)-(D) ("D" for Deselect).

To view the Selections palette:

- From the View menu, choose the Show Selections command.

   To hide the Selections palette, you can choose the Hide Selections command from the View menu, or simply click the X in the upper-right corner of the palette.

UNDERSTANDING THE SELECTION TOOLS

Using the Object Selection Tool

Not really a selection tool in the strictest
sense of the word, the Object selection tool is
really just a tool for moving things around.
The Object selection tool is used to move an
image or a selected portion of an image
within the image *canvas* (the area that contains the image and all of its elements). If
nothing is selected, the entire image will be
moved within the canvas, cutting off parts of
the image and revealing the blank white canvas underneath.

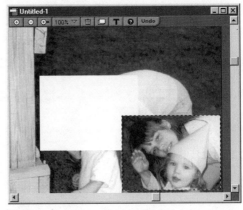

Figure 9.4 Pressing and dragging lets you move parts
of an image to different areas.

To move an image or selection:

1. If desired, select the portion of the image
   that you want to move.

2. Choose Object Selection Tool from the
   drop-down list in the Selections palette or
   choose Select > Selection Tools > Object.

3. Press and drag within the image to
   move the image or the selected area
   (**Figure 9.4**).

   With the Object selection tool active, the
   cursor does not have to be within the
   selected area.

Figure 9.5 A simple selection made using the Rectangle selection tool.

Selecting with Basic Shapes

The Rectangle, Oval, Square, and Circle selection tools all work in the exact same fashion and so are dealt with here as one type of tool. All are used to create the simplest of selections.

To select a shape area:

1. Choose any of the four basic shape selection tools (Rectangle, Oval, Square, or Circle) from within the Selections palette or from the Selection Tools submenu in the Select menu.

2. Position the crosshair cursor at one corner of the area you want to select.

3. Press and drag to the diagonally opposite corner of the area you want to select, surrounding the desired area with a basic shape selection (**Figure 9.5**).

✔ Tip

■ When creating any basic shape selection, hold down the (Alt) key to create the shape from the center outward, instead of from one corner to the other. This is especially useful when you need to center a selection on an object or person.

SELECTING WITH BASIC SHAPES

Selecting Polygonal Shapes

The Polygon selection tool is used to create angular selections, such as triangles, stars, and "new and improved" starbursts. The Polygon tool is easy to use, requiring nothing more than a click for each angle of your shape. PhotoDeluxe will connect the dots for you.

To select a polygonal area:

1. Choose Polygon Tool from the drop-down list in the Selections palette or choose Polygon from the Selection Tools sub-menu in the Select menu.

2. Click within your image to designate the starting location of the polygonal shape.

3. Move the mouse to the next point and click again. Repeat this process to create any polygonal shape.

4. When you are finished, click back on your original starting point or double-click to have PhotoDeluxe close the polygon for you (**Figure 9.6**).

✔ Tip

■ You can also press and drag with the Polygon tool to add freeform areas to your polygon (that is, lines that are not perfectly straight).

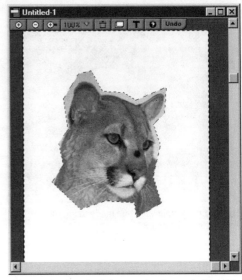

Figure 9.6 Using the Polygon selection tool, this cat's face becomes a dynamic element for later use.

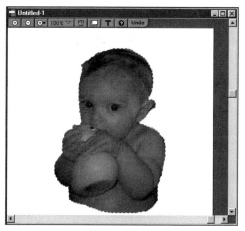

Figure 9.7 This little girl has been traced and is ready to be copied and pasted into another image.

Tracing Image Sections

For unusual shapes or intricate selections, tracing by hand is often the best solution. While neither fast nor especially exciting, manual tracing does give you absolute control of your selection. Keep in mind that even with the steadiest of hands, the mouse is not an ideal tracing device, so you will undoubtedly end up using the Add and Reduce variations to fine-tune your selection. If you think you will do a lot of tracing, you can always invest $100–200 in a stylus—a pen-like input device for computer graphics. (Wacom makes the best ones out there and has many selections for both Macintosh and PC users.)

To select a freeform area:

1. Choose Trace Tool from the drop-down list in the Selections palette or choose Trace from the Selection Tools submenu in the Select menu.

2. Move the cursor to the edge of the image element you want to trace.

3. Carefully press and drag around the object (**Figure 9.7**).

✔ Tip

■ It is with the Trace tool, more than any other tool, that you will use the Add and Reduce variations. Tracing can be a very delicate and often frustrating process. Don't worry if you make mistakes and select extra areas or leave out wanted areas. Simply use the Add variation of the Trace tool to trace around areas you missed, or use the Reduce variation to trace around unwanted areas.

Using the Color Wand

The Color Wand is everyone's favorite selection tool (at least, among those surveyed who expressed a preference). With a few simple clicks, you can use it to select an entire sky, ocean, grassy field, or interior wall. It's without a doubt the quickest way to select most backgrounds.

The Color Wand works by looking at the color of the pixel you initially click, and then selecting all contiguous (connected) pixels of a similar color.

To select color-specific areas:

1. Choose Color Wand from the drop-down list in the Selections palette or from the Selection Tools submenu in the Select menu.

2. Click in the area that you want to select.

3. Unless the area is all one color, click on the Add variation of the Color Wand and click in an adjacent area to add to the selection. Continue this process until you are happy with the selection (**Figure 9.8**).

Figure 9.8 The background of this castle was selected and deleted using the Color Wand.

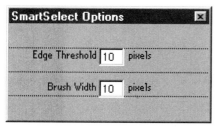

Figure 9.9 The SmartSelect Options palette lets you set the sensitivity and search area for the SmartSelect tool.

Using the SmartSelect Tool

Easily the most complicated of all the selection tools, the SmartSelect tool is also the most powerful. It works by comparing differences in color along an edge that you define. You define the edge by simply moving the mouse near it. As long as you move the mouse approximately along this edge and as long as the colors of the edge provide enough contrast, the SmartSelect tool will create a perfect selection for you. While this doesn't work with all images, it can be a huge time-saver. Even where it doesn't work one hundred percent correctly, it can still do the bulk of your work for you, leaving you with only clean-up work using the Trace tool's Add or Reduce variations.

To trace image shapes:

1. Choose SmartSelect Tool from the drop-down list in the Selections palette or choose SmartSelect from the Selection Tools submenu in the Select menu.

2. Set the Edge Threshold and Brush Width as desired in the SmartSelect Options palette that appears (**Figure 9.9**).

   Edge Threshold determines how sensitive SmartSelect is to color differences. Higher values (from 1 to 100) make the tool more sensitive.

   Brush Width determines how far from the cursor the tool looks to find color differences. Higher values (from 1 to 20) mean a broader search.

3. Move the mouse (*don't* press and drag) along the edge of the element that you want selected.

(continues on next page)

As the SmartSelect tool traces the image element, it will create points along the selection. To back up, move the mouse back to the last point. To remove the last point, press the (Delete) or (Backspace) key.

4. To finish tracing, click again on the starting point or double-click to have PhotoDeluxe close the selection for you (**Figure 9.10**).

The traced area is converted to a selection, which can be used as you would use any other selection.

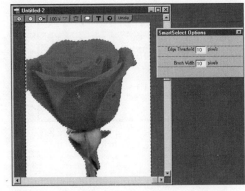

Figure 9.10 This rose, with its dark color against a lighter background, was an ideal candidate for the SmartSelect tool.

COMBINING IMAGES | 10

Images can be combined easily in PhotoDeluxe to create composite images for a wide variety of uses. You can add a more interesting background to a photograph, combine photographs of all of your relatives for a "family reunion" portrait, add humorous clip art to images, and much more.

The key to creating composite images is to understand and use layers effectively. Conceptually, layers act as sheets of clear plastic, upon which you can place photographs or other images, parts of images, text, or special effects. These sheets of clear plastic are then stacked on top of each other so that you can see through the empty parts of one sheet to the sheet below it. Thus, you could place a pumpkin head on one sheet (that is, on one layer), and a photo of your friend on the sheet (layer) below it, so that when you view or print the composite image, it appears that your friend has a pumpkin head. This is, of course, just one incredibly, hysterically funny example of what you can do with layers.

Working with Layers

Layers are displayed and manipulated using the Layers palette. The Layers palette is also used to create new layers, delete unwanted layers, and change layer options, such as layer name, opacity, and blending mode.

The Layers palette consists of a separate row for each layer in your image, starting with a Text layer. This Text layer is always present, even if your image contains no text. It is where any text you create goes. Each row in the palette has an eyeball icon you can click to show or hide that layer. Next to the eyeball is a thumbnail version of the layer contents, followed by the name of the layer. Single-clicking any layer in the palette selects it as the active layer, and any editing or other actions will affect only the active layer. Double-clicking a layer opens a dialog box with options for that layer.

At the bottom of the Layers palette are two icons: a page and a trash can. The page icon is the New Layer icon, which you click to create a new, blank layer. Click the trash icon to delete the active layer.

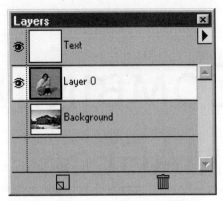

Figure 10.1 The Layers palette shows all layers in the file and includes two buttons (at the bottom) for creating new layers and deleting unwanted layers.

To show the Layers palette:

◆ From the View menu, select the Show Layers command.

This reveals the all-important Layers palette (**Figure 10.1**).

To create a layer:

1. In the Layers palette, click on the layer above which you want the new layer to appear.

This step is completely optional, since it is ridiculously easy to rearrange layers, as discussed in "To move a layer."

2. Click the New Layer button at the bottom of the Layers palette (it looks like a pad of paper with one corner folded over).

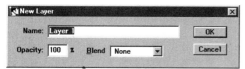

Figure 10.2 The New Layer dialog box.

3. In the New Layer dialog box that appears (**Figure 10.2**), enter a name for this new layer, and (if desired) enter an Opacity and select a Blend mode.

   Opacity simply determines how transparent the layer is. 100% opacity means that you cannot see through the image areas of the layer at all, and 0% opacity makes the entire layer completely transparent (which is sort of pointless). By altering the opacity of your layers, you can create some very nice effects, as discussed in Chapter 13, *Special Effects and Filters*.

   Blend mode determines how this layer will interact with the layers beneath it. Blend modes provide a sort of transparency, but with a twist. The different blend modes compare the color values of the underlying layers with this layer and then choose (depending on the blend mode that you have selected) which color (or combination of colors) to display. For examples of each blending mode, see the comparison of blending modes and opacity settings in the color section.

4. Click the OK button to close this dialog box.

✔ Tips

- You can create an exact copy of a layer by simply pressing on the layer you want to copy and dragging it down onto the New Layer button. The newly created layer will be an exact copy of the old layer and will be named "<old layer name> copy." This technique can be used to create a "working" copy of a layer for isolating parts of an image or applying special effects, leaving the original layer intact in case you make a mistake.

- You can change layer options at any time by simply double-clicking the desired layer.

WORKING WITH LAYERS

To delete a layer:

◆ In the Layers palette, click on the layer that you want to delete and then click the Trash button at the bottom of the Layers palette.

   You can also simply drag the unwanted layer down onto the Trash button.

To move a layer:

◆ In the Layers palette, press on the layer that you want to move and drag it up or down to the desired location in the layer stack.

   A dark horizontal border will appear as you drag the layer. When this border is in the right place release the mouse button (**Figure 10.3**).

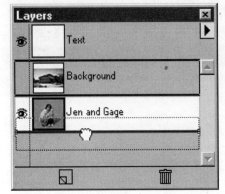

Figure 10.3 The darker horizontal line between layers shows the destination of the layer being moved.

Blend Modes

No Blend This image consists of a background of balloons with a beach scene placed over half of the image. With no blend mode, the beach scene covers the balloon background.

Color Blending based on color preserves the lightness of the background, but uses the hue and saturation of the foreground, and is useful for colorizing black and white images.

Darken The darken blend mode preserves the darkest pixels from both the background and foreground layers.

Lighten The opposite of darken, the lighten blend mode preserves the lighter pixels from both the foreground and background layers.

Difference The most colorful of the blending modes, the difference blending mode uses the red, green, and blue values of both layers to merge the two images together.

Overlay The overlay blending mode retains as much information as possible from both layers, without changing color values (as opposed to the difference mode, which does change colors dramatically).

Colorizing – Cutout

Color We started with a full-color version of an image with some good candidates for cutout elements (in this case, the yellow tree).

Gray Cutout After creating a duplicate layer, we convert the new layer to black and white, then carefully erase the tree from the image.

Final This reveals the underlying color image of the tree, creating this dramatic combination of a grayscale image with a single color element. We could carry this a step further by creating a color cutout of the truck as well.

Colorizing – Overlay

Original This great black-and-white photo is a perfect candidate for colorization, since it contains easily defined areas that we can work with. In this case, we will use different colors for the eyes, skin, hair and shirt.

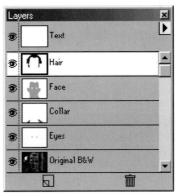

Layers Palette Create new, blank layers for each element we want to color and name the layers to keep track of which layer is which.

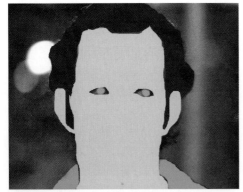

No Blends or Opacity After painting over each element of the photo, we end up with color overlays for the eyes, skin, hair, and shirt.

Colorized After adjusting the opacity and blend mode for each of our layers, we end up with this colorized version of our original photo.

Effects Sampler

To give you an idea of just some of the special effects that can be created with PhotoDeluxe's filters, here are some samples of different filters applied to an image. The effects shown here represent fewer than half of the effect filters available in PhotoDeluxe.

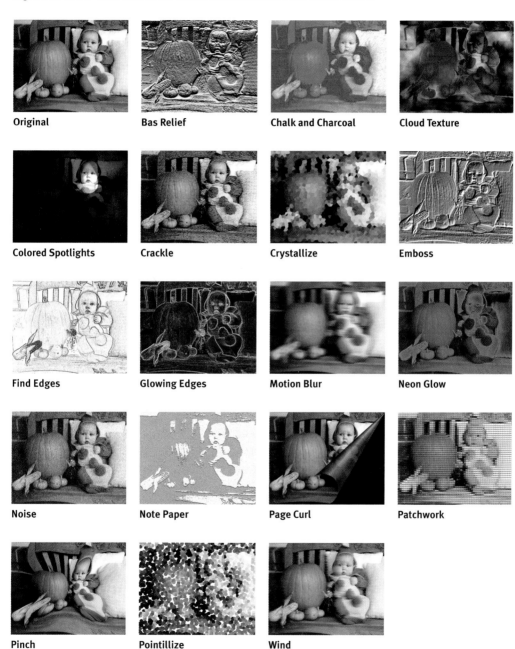

Original

Bas Relief

Chalk and Charcoal

Cloud Texture

Colored Spotlights

Crackle

Crystallize

Emboss

Find Edges

Glowing Edges

Motion Blur

Neon Glow

Noise

Note Paper

Page Curl

Patchwork

Pinch

Pointillize

Wind

Opacity

To demonstrate the difference in opacity values when combining images, we've added three colored boxes and a text block to this image of a girl playing under a sprinkler. Each colored box is on a layer of its own, as are the text block and the background image.

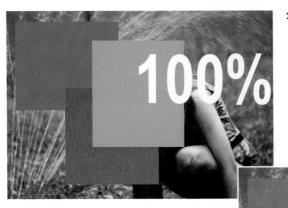

100% Opacity

75% Opacity

50% Opacity

25% Opacity

Removing Redeye

Redeye Before While a great picture of a very cute baby, this image is marred by a very distinct redeye effect.

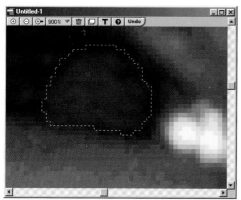

Magnified and Selected To correct the problem, magnify each eye and carefully select the red portions of the eye are using a combination of the Magic Wand and Lasso selection tools.

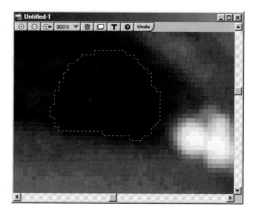

Values Changed Once selected, adjust the color values of the red portions of the eye using the Hue/Saturation command in the Quality menu.

After Correction Technically speaking, the redeye hasn't been removed as much as it has been converted to an acceptable color. Regardless, the effect is the same and this image is now ready to send out to friends and family.

Variations

Variations Dialog Box The Variations dialog box lets you adjust the color in an image by choosing from one of several, well, variations. Each time you pick a variation, you are presented with new variations of the variation you picked. This allows you to simply click and explore all of the possible color variations of your original image.

Creating a Soft Edge

Before A lovely wedding photo for a lovely couple.

After This feathered background was created by creating an oval selection around the bride and groom, feathering the selection (using the Feather command in the Effects menu), inverting the selection (using the Invert command in the Select menu), and then deleting the contents of the selection.

Correcting Dark Images

Before This poor-quality photo of two tragically dressed boys needs a lot of work. Rather than trying to fix the image manually, we will use the Extensis Instant Fix filter (in the Effects menu).

After Instant Fix did a remarkable job with this photo, lightening and sharpening the image considerably, as well as making other less-noticeable improvements. It's not perfect, but for a single click clean-up, we certainly can't complain.

Special Effects and Changing Colors

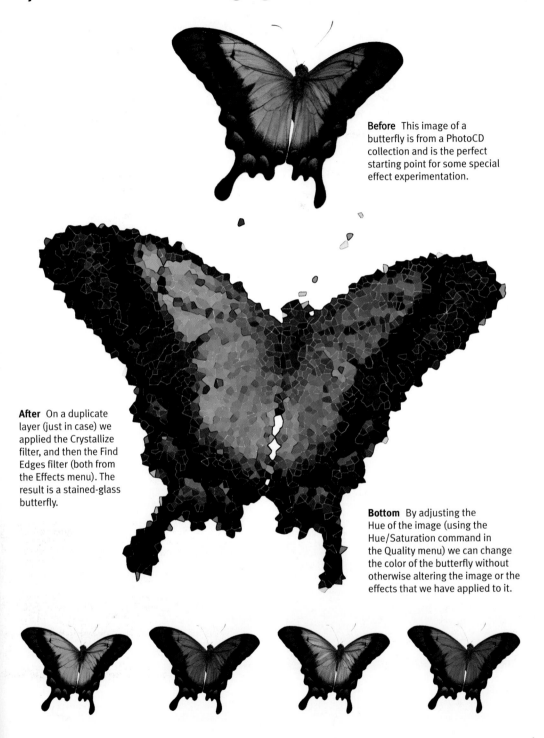

Before This image of a butterfly is from a PhotoCD collection and is the perfect starting point for some special effect experimentation.

After On a duplicate layer (just in case) we applied the Crystallize filter, and then the Find Edges filter (both from the Effects menu). The result is a stained-glass butterfly.

Bottom By adjusting the Hue of the image (using the Hue/Saturation command in the Quality menu) we can change the color of the butterfly without otherwise altering the image or the effects that we have applied to it.

Figure 10.4 The sandy background has been selected using a combination of Magic Wand and Trace selection tools.

Figure 10.5 The same image, after the background has been deleted and the canvas has been trimmed.

Isolating Image Elements

Placing one image on top of another does nothing but cover up the underlying image. To make composite images work, you need to isolate elements of an image from the image background, so you can place just the desired elements on another image. The easiest way to do this is often to delete the unwanted background portions of an image by carefully selecting and then deleting the background.

To isolate part of an image:

1. Open the file that contains the element that you want to use, and choose Save As from the File menu to save the file under a different name. Because you will be deleting large portions of this file, it is important that you *not* work on the original file.

2. Using any of the selection tools discussed in Chapter 9, select the portions of the image that you do *not* want to keep (**Figure 10.4**). If it is easier, you can also select the part of the image that you do want to keep, and then either click the Invert button in the Selections palette or choose Invert from the Select menu.

3. Press the Delete or Backspace key to delete the selected areas, leaving you with just the part of the image that you want.

4. Choose Trim from the Size menu.

5. Press and drag to create a box surrounding your remaining image.

6. If necessary, drag any of the corner handles to resize the box so that it exactly fits your remaining image.

7. Click outside of the trim box. PhotoDeluxe trims the area outside of the box, leaving you with a file canvas that is just big enough to display the image (**Figure 10.5**).

8. Save the file.

Creating Composite Images

Normally, a PhotoDeluxe file contains only a single image. To create composite images, however, you have to add images from other files. These images are added to the destination file as additional layers, which can be moved, resized, or otherwise manipulated independently to create an effective composition.

To add an image to a file:

1. Open the destination file.

2. Open the file (or files) that contain the image elements that you want to add to your destination file.

3. With the Object selection tool, drag the image you wish to add out of its window and onto the destination window (**Figure 10.6**).

   The image appears on top of the existing image in the destination file, and a new layer has been added to the Layers palette to hold the new image.

4. Select the new image and resize or rotate, as desired.

5. In the Layers palette, rename the new layer (if desired) and move the layer up or down in the layer stack to position the new image behind any foreground elements.

6. Repeat steps 2 through 5 to add additional images from other files.

Figure 10.6 Dragging an image from one window to another copies the image onto a new layer in the destination image.

Inserting New Image Elements

A very effective technique that you can use when creating composite images is to "insert" one image into another, rather than simply placing it on top of the other image. This can create the illusion that the inserted image is somehow a part of the scene.

The trick to this technique is to create a duplicate of your image layer and delete everything in the duplicate layer except for the foreground objects. You then add the additional image element between these two layers, so the new element appears to be between the foreground objects and the image background.

To insert an element into an image:

1. Open the destination image (the image that the element will be inserted into), if it is not already open.

2. In the Layers palette, drag the image layer (usually Layer 0) to the New Layer icon at the bottom of the Layers palette.

   This creates a duplicate layer called "Layer 0 copy" (or whatever the layer was called, plus "copy"). This new layer is automatically selected.

3. Hide the original image layer by clicking the eyeball icon next to it in the Layers palette.

4. Select and delete the background of the duplicate layer (Layer 0 copy).

   This will isolate the main elements of your image. You can now slip a new image or image element between these two layers.

5. Open the file that contains the image element you want to add.

(continues on next page)

6. If necessary, move the image window of the new file so that you can see at least part of the destination image window.

7. Drag the layer that contains the element to be moved out of the Layers palette and onto the destination image window.

8. In the destination image window, resize and move the object into place.

9. In the Layers palette, drag the inserted object layer between the background layer (Layer 0) and the foreground layer (Layer 0 copy) (**Figure 10.7**).

Figure 10.7 Sandwiching an image between foreground and background versions of a file creates the illusion that the inserted image is part of the scene (at least, it does when you don't use a disembodied cartoon monster head).

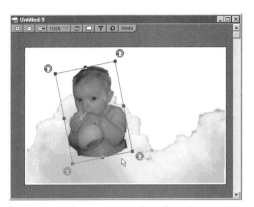

Figure 10.8 Before we can combine these images they need to be resized and rotated using the handles shown.

Rotating and Resizing Images

In the Guided Activities section, you may have resized or rotated images as part of an activity. Here, you'll learn how to resize or rotate images on your own. These skills are critical when creating composite images, as the likelihood of two or more images or image elements fitting together perfectly is pretty slim. By resizing and rotating image elements, you can combine elements from vastly different sources.

To rotate or resize an image:

1. Choose Object Selection Tool from the drop-down list in the Selections palette.

   If the Selections palette is not visible, choose Show Selections from the View menu.

2. Click on the image object that you want to work with.

   The object will be surrounded by a border, eight square resizing handles, and four round rotation handles (**Figure 10.8**).

3. To resize the object, press on any of the square resizing handles and drag in towards the center of the object to reduce the size of the object, or outward to increase the size of the object.

   Dragging a *corner* handle resizes the object while maintaining correct proportions. Dragging a *side* handle increases or decreases only the width of the object, distorting its proportions. Dragging a *top* or *bottom* handle also distorts the object, by changing only the object's height.

   (continues on next page)

ROTATING AND RESIZING IMAGES

4. To rotate the object, drag any of the circular handles outside the four corners of the object in either a clockwise or counterclockwise direction. (With the rotation handles, unlike the resizing handles, all of the handles work the exact same way.)

5. Once the object is resized and rotated, drag the middle of the object to place it as desired (**Figure 10.9**).

Once placed, you can continue to resize and rotate as needed.

Figure 10.9 The final composite, after resizing and rotating the images.

Figure 10.10
When selecting backgrounds, you will have to use the Add variations of both the Color Wand (shown here) and the Trace selection tools.

Swapping Backgrounds

One of the most common reasons to combine images is to replace an existing background. Gray, drab skies can be replaced with puffy clouds against a brilliant blue background, or busy scenes can be replaced with something more subtle so that the important foreground image elements stand out.

Swapping backgrounds is one of the simplest forms of combining images.

To swap an image's background:

1. Open the image with the background you want to replace.

2. Choose Color Wand from the drop-down list in the Selections palette.

   If the Selections palette is not visible, choose Show Selections from the View menu.

3. Click to select part of the background.

4. Click the Add button in the Selections palette (**Figure 10.10**) to add to the selection using the Color Wand.

5. Click additional areas of your background to add them to the selection.

6. If necessary, use additional selection tools to select any unselected areas of your background.

   We find that the Add variation of the Trace tool works best here, as it allows you to simply drag a loop around unselected areas to add them to the selection.

7. Once you have your background selected, press the Delete or Backspace key to delete the selected area of your image.

8. Click the None button in the Selections palette to remove the selection.

(continues on next page)

9. Open the image that contains the background you want to use.

10. Drag the background image onto the foreground image.

This adds a new layer to the foreground image that contains the new background. This new layer appears above the foreground image layer, however.

11. In the Layers palette, drag the new layer below the original layer to move the background to its appropriate place in the background (**Figures 10.11 and 10.12**).

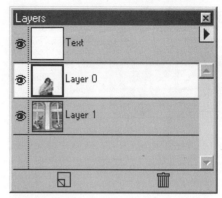

Figure 10.11 The Layers palette of our composite image shows the isolated subject layer above the new background layer.

Figure 10.12 Mother and son in front of a picturesque window scene, instead of a boring background.

TEXTURES
AND BACKGROUNDS

No matter what type of image you are working with, it can probably be improved at least somewhat by adding a little texture or by playing with the background. This chapter discusses numerous techniques for enhancing images using these two related topics.

Textures can be used to add realism, interest, or contrast to images, whether by adding "stucco" to walls, creating cloudy skies, or using "hidden identity" camera effects, or by blurring or colorizing backgrounds, adding drop shadows, or even curling the corner of your image.

Most of the techniques discussed in this chapter do make use of PhotoDeluxe's layering capabilities, so we recommend having read through Chapter 10, *Combining Images*, before working in this chapter.

Creating Stucco Textures

The stucco texture technique that you are about to learn is a great example of what can be accomplished by combining filter effects to create new or more convincing texture effects than those created using just a single filter. This effect can be used to add texture, that is, depth and interest, to large, flat areas of color. It is obviously ideal for buildings and such, but can also be used to add texture to just about any image surface.

To create a stucco texture:

1. Open the file you want to work in and select the portions of the image to which you want to apply the stucco texture.

2. Choose the Noise command from the Noise sub-menu in the Effects menu.

3. In the Noise dialog box (**Figure 11.1**), select the Gaussian Distribution option and select the Monochromatic checkbox.

4. Click the OK button.

5. Choose the Crackle command from the Texture sub-menu in the Effects menu.

6. In the Crackle dialog box (**Figure 11.2**), adjust the Crack Spacing, Crack Depth, and Crack Brightness settings, if desired. (The default settings work well here.)

7. Click the OK button to complete the effect (**Figure 11.3**).

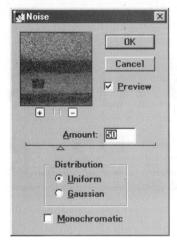

Figure 11.1
The Noise dialog box is used to add texture to the image areas for further manipulation.

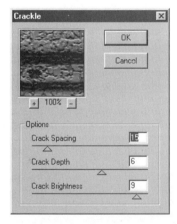

Figure 11.2
The Crackle dialog box is what makes the stucco effect work.

Figure 11.3 In this finished image, the low wall on the right has our new "stucco" applied to it.

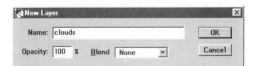

Figure 11.4 Name the new layer using the New Layer dialog box.

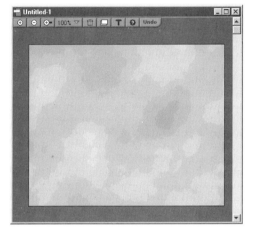

Figure 11.5 PhotoDeluxe creates random cloud textures using the current foreground and background colors.

Creating Cloud Textures

The two cloud texture filters are used to create very different effects. The Clouds filter simply creates a cloud-like texture using the current foreground and background colors (typically blue and white). The Cloud Texture filter, on the other hand, uses the same texture as the Clouds filter, but then blends this texture with the existing image colors to create an unusual effect, as you will see.

To create clouds:

1. If the Layers palette is not already visible, choose the Show Layers command from the View menu.

2. Click the New Layer icon at the bottom of the Layers palette.

3. In the New Layer dialog box that appears, name this new layer "clouds" (or something to that effect), and then click the OK button (**Figure 11.4**).

   A new, blank layer is created above the previously selected layer. For more information on creating and working with layers, see Chapter 10, *Combining Images*.

4. From the Effects menu, select the Clouds command in the Render sub-menu.

   The new "clouds" layer is filled with white clouds against a blue background (**Figure 11.5**).

5. If you want to be able to see through the clouds layer to the underlying layer, double-click the clouds layer in the Layers palette and reduce the opacity to 25% or so in the Layer Options dialog box (experiment with different settings until you are happy with the result).

✔ Tips

■ The Clouds filter can be used with any two colors, not just blue and white. The Clouds filter only happens to create natural-looking clouds because the default foreground and background colors are blue and white. By changing the foreground and background colors, you could just as easily create red clouds against a black background, or any other color combination. Change foreground and background colors using the Choose Colors command in the Effects menu. Changing colors is discussed in detail in Chapter 12, *Painting*.

■ By combining this clouds technique with the swapping backgrounds techniques discussed in Chapter 10, *Combining Images*, you can easily place any image against a realistic cloudy sky.

To use the Cloud Texture effect:

1. In the Layers palette, select the layer to which you want to apply the cloud texture.

   Note: Unlike the Clouds filter, the Cloud Texture filter will *not* work on an empty layer.

2. In the Effects menu, select the Cloud Texture command from the Render sub-menu.

3. PhotoDeluxe creates a cloud texture and merges it with the selected layer (**Figure 11.6**).

   This merging creates an inverted effect that looks similar to a photographic negative. If you don't like the effect, use the Undo command to change your image back to normal. You can alter this effect considerably by changing your foreground and background colors before applying the Cloud Texture effect.

Figures 11.6 The Cloud Texture filter creates a cloud texture (see Figure 11.5) and merges it with the existing image (Figure 11.6, top), often with unexpected results (Figure 11.6, bottom).

✔ Tip

■ The closer to black your foreground and background colors are, the less of an effect the Cloud Texture filter produces. Try using a dark foreground color and black as your background color for more subtle results.

CREATING CLOUD TEXTURES

Figure 11.7 If it's good enough for television, a little anonymity is good enough for us. Here we start by selecting the face we want obscured.

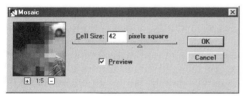

Figure 11.8 Pay attention to the preview in this dialog box as you change the settings.

Figure 11.9 Now no one will ever know who made this little girl wear those ridiculous glasses.

Using Other Texture Effects

In addition to the texture effects already discussed in this chapter, you can experiment with any of the filters in the Effects menu. Two that you might find particularly interesting are the Mosaic and Patchwork filters.

The Mosaic filter can be used for an amusing "hidden identity" effect, while the Patchwork filter is used to create true mosaic effects. And if anyone can tell us why, we'll give them a prize (not really).

But don't limit yourself to just these two filters. Experiment with other filters and combinations of other filters to discover unique effects that no one else has ever created.

To protect identities using the Mosaic filter:

1. Choose the Oval selection tool from the drop-down list in the Selections palette, or choose Oval from the Selection Tools sub-menu in the Select menu.

2. Press and drag in the image to create an oval selection around the face of the person whose identity you want to protect (**Figure 11.7**).

3. From the Effects menu, choose the Mosaic command from the Pixelate sub-menu.

4. In the Mosaic dialog box (**Figure 11.8**), increase or decrease the Cell Size setting until you are happy with the level of concealment.

5. Click the OK button to exit the dialog box and return to your image, where the selected area is now adequately obscured (**Figure 11.9**).

To make a mosaic using the Patchwork filter:

1. Choose the Patchwork command from the Texture sub-menu of the Effects menu.

2. In the Patchwork dialog box, adjust the Square Size and Depth settings as desired (**Figure 11.10**).

   For many of the filters in PhotoDeluxe, you can zoom in and out of your image using the plus and minus buttons just below the image preview. You can also pan around your image by dragging inside the image preview.

3. Click the OK button to have the Patchwork filter applied to your image (**Figure 11.11**).

Figure 11.10 As with the Mosaic filter, the preview is invaluable when adjusting the settings for the Patchwork filter.

Figure 11.11 The finished product, a mosaic created (seemingly) from hundreds of individual tiles.

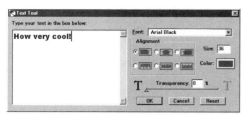

Figure 11.12 Use the Text Tool dialog box to enter text, and select a font, size, and alignment.

Using Textures with Text

PhotoDeluxe makes it easy to add text to any image by using the Text tool at the top of the image window. Text is added to a special text layer that appears above all other layers in your image. Unfortunately, you cannot apply textures or other special effects directly to this layer. Instead you must create pseudo-text effects by creating a "border" of sorts for your text. This is done by creating a layer below the text layer and filling part of this new layer with a texture.

To reverse text against a texture:

1. Click the Text button (the T) at the top of the image window.

2. In the Text Tool dialog box (**Figure 11.12**), type your text, select a font from the drop-down list, enter a size, and change the alignment and color of the text, then click the OK button.

   If, after exiting the Text Tool dialog box, you want to make adjustments to your text, just double-click the text. The dialog box will re-open and you can make any desired changes.

3. Choose the Rectangle selection tool (from either the drop-down list in the Selections palette or from the Selection Tools sub-menu in the Select menu) and create a rectangular selection around your text.

4. Choose the Clouds (*not* Cloud Texture) command from the Render sub-menu of the Effects menu.

   This fills the selected area with clouds so that you can apply a texture effect (you cannot apply texture effects to an empty selection). If you like the way it looks as is and don't want to apply additional texture effects, skip to step 6 or 7.

(continues on next page)

5. Apply any texture effect to the selection by choosing filters from the Artistic, Pixelate, or Texture sub-menus of the Effects menu.

Unless you have a very light texture behind your text, it will probably look better if it is reversed (white against a dark background, instead of the more common black against a light background).

6. Choose the Object selection tool (from the Selections palette drop-down list or from the Selection Tools sub-menu in the Select menu) and double-click on your text.

7. In the Text Tool dialog box, click on the Color swatch.

8. In the resulting Color Picker dialog box (**Figure 11.13**), click the white swatch in the upper-left corner of the grid of available color swatches.

9. Click the OK button to exit the Color Picker, and then click the OK button in the Text Tool dialog box to exit it as well.

The text in your image is now white against a textured background. If the background of the image is also white, it will look like the text is cut out of the texture (**Figure 11.14**).

Figure 11.13 Picking a new color is a simple matter of clicking on the desired color swatch.

Figure 11.14 Reversed text is often much more legible than regular text, especially against a dark or busy texture.

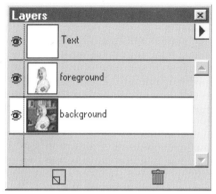

Figure 11.15 Using a separate layer for the image background (instead of just selecting the background areas) gives you much more freedom for experimenting and applying multiple effects.

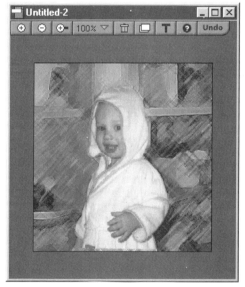

Figure 11.16 A nice effect is created by applying the Colored Pencil filter to just the background layer of this image.

Creating Textured Backgrounds

All of the texture effects that we have looked at so far in this chapter can be applied to an entire image background. By applying a texture (or any effect) to a background, but not to foreground elements, you can add interest and emphasis to the image.

Most background effects can be applied in one of two ways: by selecting the background areas of the image and applying the effect to the selection, or by creating a separate layer for the background and applying the effect to the entire background layer. We highly recommend creating a separate background layer. Not only are separate layers easier to work with, but they offer many possibilities for experimentation and combination effects that are either unwieldy or simply unavailable when working in a single layer.

To create a textured background:

1. In the Layers palette, click on the layer that you want to use as a background.

   If your foreground and background are not on separate layers, duplicate the image layer, rename the two layers "foreground" and "background" or something similar, and delete everything from the foreground layer (the top layer) except for the main image elements (**Figure 11.15**). See Chapter 10, *Combining Images*, for a detailed discussion of isolating image elements from backgrounds.

2. From the Effects menu, choose from any of the following texture filters:

   Colored Pencil, from the Artistic sub-menu, creates a hand-drawn look for the background (**Figure 11.16**).

   Noise, from the Noise sub-menu, creates a speckled background.

(continues on next page)

Crystallize, from the Pixelate menu, creates a bathroom-window/shower-door effect. (It's hard to describe any other way. Try it and you'll see for yourself.)

Pointillize, also from the Pixelate menu, creates a petri-dish sort of background effect. (Again, try it and you'll see what we mean.)

Or try any of the filters in the Sketch, Stylize, or Texture sub-menus.

3. If you don't like any of the effects, use the Undo command in the Edit menu to undo the application of the filter and then try something else.

If you want to experiment further, continue this process to apply additional filter effects.

✔ Tip

- You can drag the background layer to the New Layer icon at the bottom of the Layers palette to create multiple backgrounds, then apply different effects to each of the background layers. This way you can view the different effects by simply showing or hiding each layer in turn (click the eyeball icon next to each layer).

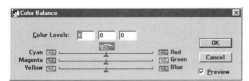

Figure 11.17 The Color Balance dialog box lets you substitute any color for the shades of gray in a black and white background.

Creating Colorized Backgrounds

In addition to creating textured backgrounds, you can create interesting background effects by simply altering or eliminating the color from your backgrounds. Making a background black and white is a simple one-step process (well, okay, two steps if you count selecting the layer as a step). You can also create duotone effects by adding a single color to a black and white background.

To create a black and white background:

1. In the Layers palette, click on the layer that you want to use as a background.

   If your foreground and background are not on separate layers, duplicate the image layer, rename the two layers "foreground" and "background" or something similar, and delete everything from the foreground layer (the top layer) except for the main image elements. See Chapter 10, *Combining Images*, for a detailed discussion of isolating image elements from backgrounds.

2. From the Effects menu, choose the Color to Black/White command. That's it!

To colorize a background:

1. Convert the background layer to black and white, as described above.

2. With the background layer still selected, choose the Color Balance command from the Quality menu.

3. In the Color Balance dialog box (**Figure 11.17**), drag the three color sliders to adjust the background color as desired.

4. Click the OK button to exit the Color Balance dialog box.

✔ Tip

- In addition to simply converting backgrounds to black and white or single colors, you can use any of PhotoDeluxe's color correction tools (Brightness, Contrast, Hue, and Saturation) to make adjustments to your image backgrounds independent of the foreground elements.

Using Gradients as Backgrounds

Gradient fills can be created easily in PhotoDeluxe and used as backgrounds for image elements. Gradients consist of a smooth blend from one color to another and can be either linear (straight line) or radial (from the center outward). Gradient backgrounds can be used for special effects or as a substitute sky background.

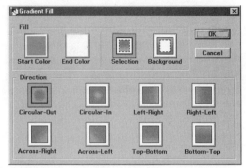

Figure 11.18 The Gradient Fill dialog box is used to fill the selection with a two-color gradient.

To add a gradient to a background:

1. In the Layers palette, click the background layer of your image.

   The gradient you are about to create will fill this layer completely. If you want to keep the existing background intact, create a new, blank layer between the existing foreground and background layers. See Chapter 10, *Combining Images*, for information on creating and moving layers.

2. From the Select menu, choose the All command or click the All button in the Selections palette.

3. From the Effects menu, choose the Gradient Fill command.

4. In the Fill section of the Gradient Fill dialog box (**Figure 11.18**), click the Start Color swatch.

5. In the resulting Color Picker dialog box (**Figure 11.19**), click on any color, then click the OK button to set the selected color as the starting color for your gradient.

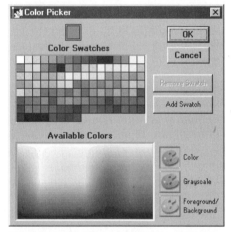

Figure 11.19 The standard Color Picker is used to choose the start and end colors for the gradient.

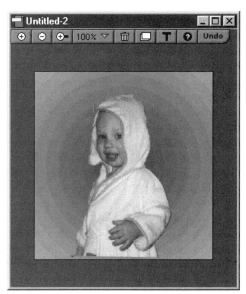

Figure 11.20 The finished image with a gradient background.

6. Click the End Color swatch.

7. Pick an ending color from the Color Picker dialog box, then click the OK button to return to the Gradient Fill dialog box.

8. Click on any of the eight Direction samples to determine the shape and angle of your gradient.

9. Click the OK button to apply the gradient to your background (**Figure 11.20**).

Creating Swirled Backgrounds

One effect that you won't use very often, but that is sure to get noticed when you do use it, is a swirled background—as if your background image were liquid and you twirled a stick through it.

To create a swirled background:

1. In the Layers palette, click to select the background layer.

2. From the Effects menu, choose the Twirl command from the Distort sub-menu.

3. In the Twirl dialog box (**Figure 11.21**), drag the Angle marker all the way to the right or the left (depending on whether you want your background to swirl clockwise or counterclockwise).

4. Click the OK button to apply the Twirl filter to your background (**Figure 11.22**).

Figure 11.21 The Twirl filter at its maximum setting is used to create our swirled background.

Figure 11.22 The final image with a swirled background creates a psychedelic effect.

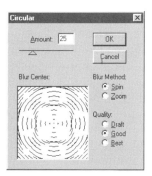

Figure 11.23
The Circular blur dialog box lets you fine-tune spin or zoom blur effects.

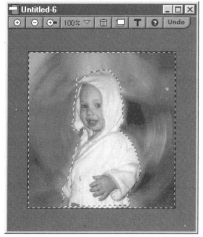

Figure 11.24 The Circular blur makes the background seem to spin around this little boy.

Figure 11.25 Use this double-vision blur effect for your whole image for those photos of your next New Year's Eve party.

Blurring Backgrounds

Good photographs, especially portraits, often have a shallow depth of field so that the subject of the photo is in sharp focus but the rest of the photograph is slightly or drastically blurred. This forces the eye to the subject of the photograph. If you didn't think about this very effective technique when you were taking your photos, don't worry. You can easily blur a background using PhotoDeluxe's various blur filter effects.

To blur an image background:

1. Select the image's background layer by clicking it in the Layers palette.

2. From the Effects menu, choose any of the commands in the Blur sub-menu.

   Blur performs a quick blur of the selected layer or image area.

   Blur More creates a more intense blur.

   Circular creates a circular blur to simulate the effect of an object being photographed while spinning (the Spin option) or while moving toward or away from the camera (the Zoom option).

   Motion Blur creates a bi-directional blur at any angle to simulate the blurring of an object when photographed in motion.

   Soften creates a blur effect of adjustable intensity.

3. For the Circular, Motion Blur, and Soften blurs, adjust the settings in the dialog box as desired (**Figure 11.23**), then click the OK button to apply the blur effect to your background (**Figure 11.24**).

✔ Tip

■ For a *great* double-vision blur effect, use the Fragment filter found in the Pixelate sub-menu of the Effects menu (**Figure 11.25**).

BLURRING BACKGROUNDS

Curling Photograph Corners

Almost all of the filters in the Effects menu can be used in a variety of different ways. Either they can be applied to different image areas, or with different settings, or they can even be combined with other filters. Not so for the most recognizable one-trick pony in the entire computer graphics industry: the page curl.

The Page Curl filter applies a unique graphic effect to your image, creating the illusion of a page curling up at the corner. This effect is beautifully done, but has unfortunately been over-used in print and Web graphics.

Figure 11.26 The very cool, but all-too-often-over-used, Page Curl effect.

To curl the corner of a photograph:

1. Select the layer that you want to curl by clicking it in the Layers palette.

2. Choose the Page Curl command from the PhotoDeluxe sub-menu of the Effects menu.

3. The Page Curl effect is applied to your image, with the current foreground color filling the area "behind" the page (**Figure 11.26**).

✔ Tip

■ If you want the page curl to reveal something on the underlying "page," just use the Color Wand to select the fill color, then press the Backspace or Delete key. The fill color will be removed to reveal the image on the layer below the layer containing the page curl.

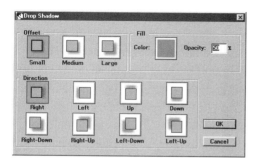

Figure 11.27 The Drop Shadow dialog box lets you customize your drop shadows to fit your image compositions.

Creating Depth with Shadows

One way to enhance the three-dimensional aspect of your images is to add a drop shadow to foreground elements, giving your image composition the illusion of depth.

PhotoDeluxe makes it very easy to add drop shadows to image elements. The only real drawback to PhotoDeluxe drop shadows is that they tend to have very sharply defined edges, and so are often not immediately appropriate for photographic images. This can be remedied, however, by combining the drop shadow technique with the previously discussed activity for blurring background layers (substituting the drop shadow layer for the background layer, of course).

To add a shadow to an image:

1. Select the image element to which you want to apply a shadow.

    If the image element is already isolated on a layer of its own, select the layer in the Layers palette, click in the empty areas of the layer with the Color Wand, and then click the Invert button in the Selections palette.

2. From the Effects menu, choose the Drop Shadow command.

3. In the Drop Shadow dialog box (**Figure 11.27**), click on Small, Medium, or Large in the Offset section to choose the distance from the edge of your object to the edge of the shadow.

4. In the Direction section, click on one of the angles for your shadow.

(continues on next page)

5. If you want a different shadow color, click on the Color swatch in the Fill area and then click a color in the Color Picker dialog box that appears. You can also adjust the opacity of the shadow.

6. Click the OK button to exit the Drop Shadow dialog box and return to your image (**Figure 11.28**).

✔ Tip

■ To soften the edges of your drop shadows, use the Blur or Blur More filters. Softening shadows makes them look more realistic, especially when adding drop shadows to photographs.

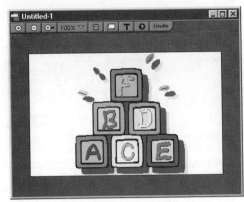

Figure 11.28 A little bit of a drop shadow adds depth and interest to this clip art image.

CREATING DEPTH WITH SHADOWS

PAINTING

PhotoDeluxe has several painting tools that you can use to add color or other effects to an image. These tools include regular brushes for painting in the color of your choice, erasers for removing painted effects or portions of an image, text and line tools for adding text and text call-outs to an image, and smudge and clone tools for altering the appearance of an image.

All of these tools affect a single layer at a time, so it is important that you have at least a basic understanding of how to create and delete layers before beginning this chapter. Layers are covered in Chapter 10, *Combining Images*.

Understanding the Painting Tools

All of the painting tools can be found in the Tools menu and most of them work in a very similar fashion. (The Text and Line tools are the exceptions.) This section is designed to get you comfortable with basic painting techniques, such as choosing a brush size, picking a color, and actually painting on an image.

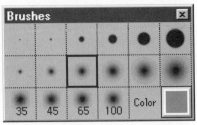

Figure 12.1 The Brushes palette consists of different brush sizes and a brush color swatch.

To paint on an image:

1. Create a new blank image or open an existing image.

2. In the Layers palette, click the New Layer icon to create a new layer. Name the new layer "paint" or something similar.

   We recommend always painting on an empty layer. If you paint on the layer that contains your image, you will be forever altering the image (unless you immediately choose Undo or close the file without saving changes). If, however, you paint on an empty layer, you can experiment, or make changes or corrections, all on the empty layer. The net effect is the same, since the empty paint layer appears above the image layer, but the process is far safer. And, by painting on a separate layer, you give yourself the option of creating interesting effects using layer opacity and blending modes, as discussed later in this chapter.

3. From the Tools menu, choose the Brush command.

   This will display the Brushes palette (**Figure 12.1**).

4. Select a brush size by clicking on one of the sample sizes in the Brushes palette.

   The top row contains hard-edged brushes, the middle and bottom rows contain

Figure 12.2 Clicking any color here sets that color as the new brush color.

Figure 12.3 Painting in PhotoDeluxe is just like painting in real life, only without the mess.

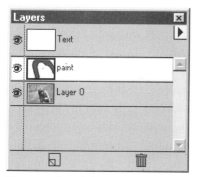

Figure 12.4 By painting on a separate layer, your original image remains intact.

soft-edged (feathered) brushes. The numbers in the bottom row represent the diameter (in pixels) of larger brushes.

5. Click on the Color swatch in the lower-right corner of the Brushes palette to activate the Color Picker (**Figure 12.2**).

6. In the Color Picker, click on any of the color swatches or click in any area in the Available Colors section to make that color the new foreground color (and thus, the color of your paintbrush).

7. Click the OK button in the Color Picker to return to your image.

8. Make sure that the "paint" layer is the active layer (it should already be, but you can click on it in the Layers palette to be sure) and press and drag in the image window to paint with your chosen brush and color (**Figure 12.3**).

9. In the Brushes palette, select other brush sizes and colors, and continue painting in your image.

10. Notice the Layers palette. The painting is actually being applied to the "paint" layer, not to the actual image layer (**Figure 12.4**). Hide the "paint" layer (by clicking the eyeball icon to the left of the paint layer in the Layers palette) to hide all painted effects.

✔ Tip

■ For complex painted effects, you can use several painting layers (one for each color or brush size, or for different painted elements) or one layer for borders and another for fills, and so on. By using multiple painting layers, you will be able to rearrange painted effects, as well as more easily edit or correct painted areas.

UNDERSTANDING THE PAINTING TOOLS

Erasing Image Areas and Effects

The Eraser tool works identically to the Brush tool, but instead of adding color, the Eraser tool removes all color from the selected areas. In a multi-layer image, erasing from an upper layer reveals the contents of the layer or layers underneath.

To erase part of an image or effect:

1. From the Tools menu, choose the Eraser command.

   This brings up the Erasers palette (**Figure 12.5**), which looks and works like the Brushes palette, but does not include a Color swatch.

2. Click on any of the sample erasers in the Erasers palette to choose an eraser size and style.

   The top row of erasers have a sharply defined edge, while the bottom two rows have a softer, feathered edge.

3. In the Layers palette, click on the layer that contains the image elements or effects that you want to erase.

   Choose Show Layers from the View menu if the Layers palette is not visible.

4. Press and drag in the image window to erase the unwanted portions of the selected layer (**Figure 12.6**).

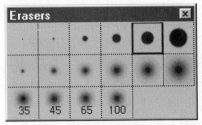

Figure 12.5 The Erasers palette contains both sharp- and soft-edged erasers.

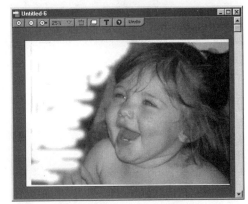

Figure 12.6 Pressing and dragging the mouse button erases unwanted portions of the selected image layer.

Figure 12.7 The sampling point determines the source for the cloning brush (the area of the image that you paint with).

Cloning Image Areas

If you are looking for some oohs and aahs from family and friends, just sit them down and show them how easy it is to "airbrush" out unwanted items from their photos, such as people or those unsightly freckles, blemishes, and tattoos. You can also use PhotoDeluxe's cloning tool to add elements, creating a third eye in the middle of dear old mom's forehead, or grafting an extra set of arms onto the baby.

The process of cloning is a fairly simple one. You simply select which part of the image you want to use as your source, then you paint on the target area and the source is duplicated, brushstroke by brushstroke. It is sort of like copying your image and then brushing on portions of it (starting with a source point that you choose) somewhere else with the cloning brush.

To remove unwanted image elements:

1. Arrange your image so that the layer containing the unwanted image element is selected in the Layers palette and the image itself is centered in the image window (and magnified, if necessary).

2. From the Tools menu, choose the Clone command. The Clone palette appears, giving you different cloning brush sizes to work with, and a sampling point marker appears in the middle of the image window (**Figure 12.7**).

3. Drag the sampling point to a location in the image that is similar to what you want to replace the unwanted element with.

   The area around the sampling point will be used when you "paint" over the unwanted element with the cloning brush.

(continues on next page)

CLONING IMAGE AREAS

4. Click on an appropriate brush size in the Clone palette.

   Small brushes tend to create an obvious "stroke" effect, but allow for detail work, while large brushes are best for filling in backgrounds or painting over large elements. Also, the soft-edged brushes tend to work better, because they make the strokes less obvious.

5. Position the brush cursor (*not* the sampling point) over the unwanted image element and press and drag the mouse to "paint" over the unwanted element with the portion of the image under the sampling point (**Figure 12.8**).

   You can move the sampling point to select different source areas as you paint with the cloning brush. This can prevent an obvious duplication of an entire portion of the image.

Figures 12.8 A before (top) and after (bottom) of the clone brush in action shows how an unsightly stop sign is removed.

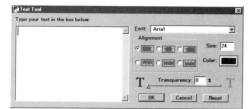

Figure 12.9 The Text Tool dialog box contains everything you need to create and format text.

Creating Text Labels

Adding a text label to an image involves the use of two simple tools: the Text tool and the Line tool. The Text tool can be accessed from either the Tools menu or from the image window toolbar (it's the T button). The Line tool can only be accessed from the Tools menu.

Text is automatically placed in the Text layer (an independent layer in every image file), but unless you remember to create a new layer for the line itself, the original image will be permanently altered—something you never want to do.

To add a text label:

1. From the Tools menu choose the Text command, or click the Text (T) button in the image window toolbar.

   Either of these actions will open the Text Tool dialog box (**Figure 12.9**).

2. Type your text, and format it as desired using the options along the right side of the dialog box.

   The *Font* pop-up menu lists all of the fonts installed on your computer.

   Click any of the *Alignment* options to choose left-, center-, or right-aligned text, with either a regular or sideways orientation.

   Enter the desired text size in the *Size* field.

   Click the *Color* swatch to choose a color from the Color Picker dialog box.

   Drag the *Transparency* slider to create varying degrees of see-through text. 0% transparency is completely opaque, while 100% transparency is invisible (and rather pointless).

(continues on next page)

CREATING TEXT LABELS

3. Click the OK button to exit the dialog box and return to your image.

   If, after seeing the text on your image, you want to make changes to the text, simply double-click on the text. This will re-open the Text Tool dialog box.

4. Move and resize the text as desired.

   Drag the middle of the text to move it and drag any of the selection handles to resize it.

5. In the Layers palette, click the New Layer icon to create a new layer. Name this new layer "line" or something similar.

6. From the Tools menu, choose the Line command.

7. In the Line Tool Options palette (**Figure 12.10**), enter a line width and (if desired) change the line color (by clicking on the Color swatch and choosing a new color in the Color Picker).

8. Position the small crosshair line cursor in the image window at the starting location of the line. Press and drag to the ending location and let go of the mouse.

   Your image is now annotated with a text label and a line pointing to specific location (**Figure 12.11**). If you should need to change the line, just select the line layer and use the Eraser and Line tools to erase the old line and draw a new one.

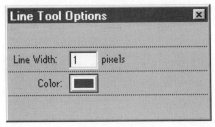

Figure 12.10 There are only two options when it comes to lines: width and color.

Figure 12.11 Use this handy, clearly labeled map if you ever get lost.

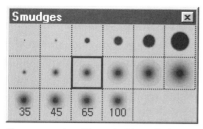

Figure 12.12 As with most of the painting tool palettes, the Smudges palette contains different brush sizes from which to choose.

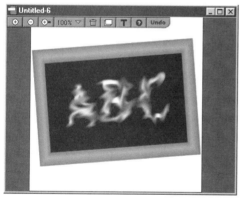

Figure 12.13 The original image (top) and after a bit of not-too-subtle smudging (bottom).

Smudging Artwork

Anyone who has ever watched a street artist work knows that drawing is only half of what makes his or her drawings look right. The other half is smudging. By smudging an image, you can blend edges to create a softer look. Smudging can also be used to create special effects, such as speed blurs or water damage.

Unlike most of the painting you've done so far in this chapter, you have to work on the image layer itself when smudging. This is because the smudge effect is calculated based on the color values of the pixels you smudge. We do, however, still encourage you to create a new layer, if only to duplicate your artwork in case you make a mistake while smudging.

To smudge an image:

1. Duplicate the layer that you want to smudge.

   To duplicate a layer, drag the layer (in the Layers palette) onto the New Layer icon. This creates a copy of the layer, places the copy directly above the original in the layer stack, and selects the copy.

2. From the Tools menu, choose the Smudge command. The Smudges palette appears (**Figure 12.12**).

3. Click on any of the brush sizes in the Smudges palette.

4. Press and drag in the image window to smudge your image (**Figure 12.13**).

   If you make a mistake, click the Undo button in the image window toolbar. If you make multiple mistakes or cannot undo, simply delete the layer you have been working with and create another copy of your original artwork layer.

   (continues on next page)

✔ Tip

■ You can create some very subtle effects with smudging and layer options, such as opacity. To create this more realistic version of the chalkboard (**Figure 12.14**), we added a new layer with a lot of additional white text, smudged it into oblivion, then changed the opacity of the new layer to 50% and the blend mode to Lighten (so that the lighter "ABC" would take precedence over our darker smudged text).

Figure 12.14 A much more realistic look is created by merging a massively smudged layer with the original using reduced opacity and the Lighten blend mode.

Figure 12.15 At 200%, this pear should be traceable, even with a mouse.

Tracing Image Elements

Before we dive into this next task, it is important to understand that this is not necessarily the best way to trace images. It's pretty much the only way to do it in PhotoDeluxe, but if you need to create a lot of accurate line art from photographic images, do yourself a huge favor and buy Adobe Streamline. This product does an excellent job of tracing complex images. (Check out www.adobe.com for more information on Streamline or other Adobe products.) If you want to trace in PhotoDeluxe, you just need to have a steady hand and a lot of patience (and this book, of course). If you do feel compelled to do a lot of tracing in PhotoDeluxe, you might want to invest in a graphics tablet and stylus, which look and act more like traditional paper and pen. In our opinion, Wacom makes the best graphics tablets on the planet, and they generally range in price from $100 to $400.

To trace over part of an image:

1. In the Layers palette, click the New Layer icon to create a new layer above your image.

2. From the Tools menu, choose the Brush command.

3. In the Brushes palette, choose a fairly small, sharp-edged brush.

4. In the image window, zoom in until you feel that you could comfortably follow the edge of the object that you want to trace (**Figure 12.15**).

5. Press and drag to trace along a small section of the image.

   Trace in short sections, so that you can easily undo mistakes. If you make a mistake that you can't undo, use the Eraser tool to erase the mistake.

(continues on next page)

TRACING IMAGE ELEMENTS

6. Save the file as you work.

7. If your image has several well-defined sections, you might want to create additional layers for each section. This will allow you to view or work with just one traced section at a time.

8. When you are done tracing, hide the original image (by clicking the eyeball in the Layers palette) (**Figure 12.16**).

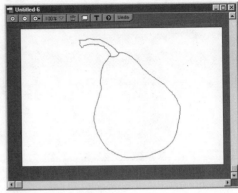

Figure 12.16 It's not perfect, but this line drawing is at least recognizable as a pear.

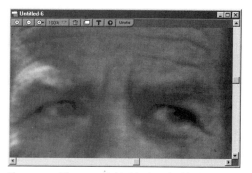

Figure 12.17 The eyes of this black and white image would look great with a little color.

Colorizing Black and White Images

In Chapter 11, *Textures and Backgrounds*, you saw a technique for colorizing images that added a color tint to an entire black and white image. Here, you'll learn how to use painting tools and layer options to add color tints to different parts of an image. Done properly, this can create dramatic effects and eye-catching images.

To colorize a black and white image:

1. If necessary, convert the image to black and white (choose Color to Black/White from the Effects menu), and save under a different name (Save As from the File menu).

2. Zoom in to the area that you want to work with (**Figure 12.17**). (Use the Zoom tool in the image window toolbar.)

3. Create a new layer. (Click the New Layer icon in the Layers palette and name the new layer according to the area or image element that you are colorizing.)

4. Choose the Brush command from the Tools menu.

5. In the Brushes palette, choose a brush size and style (hard- or soft-edged) that is appropriate for the area you will be colorizing.

6. Click the Color swatch in the Brushes palette and pick a color from the resulting Color Picker dialog box. Click OK in the Color Picker dialog box to exit.

7. Press and drag in the image window to paint over the image area or elements that you want to colorize.

(continues on next page)

8. In the Layers palette, double-click on the new colorizing layer you created to open its Layer Options dialog box (**Figure 12.18**).

9. In the Layer Options dialog box, change the Blend mode to Overlay.

   You can experiment with other blend modes. Darken also works well and produces a more subtle effect.

10. Adjust the Opacity as desired.

    We usually start with 50% and then adjust from there, if necessary.

11. Click OK to return to your image.

12. Repeat this process to create additional colorized layers for other areas of the image.

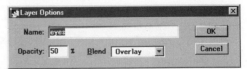

Figure 12.18 The trick to making convincing colors is to use the Opacity and Blend options in this dialog box.

SPECIAL EFFECTS & FILTERS

13

In addition to its tools and features for image correction and enhancement, PhotoDeluxe comes with a wide variety of special effect filters that enable you to create images that run the gamut from blasé to beautiful to downright bizarre. Some of these filters have already been discussed in Chapter 11, *Textures and Backgrounds*. Here, you will learn to alter your images to create patterns and edge effects, add ripples and other distortions, or convert scanned images to look like they were hand-painted. Because of the experimental nature of applying filters and discovering their effects (both good and bad), it is helpful to keep a few things in mind.

- ◆ To avoid making irreversible changes to the original image, always save the image under a different name before starting to experiment, and always create duplicate layers on which to test different filters. Once you are happy with a filter effect, you can delete unwanted or unused layers.

- ◆ After each application of a filter, use the Undo command in the Edit menu ([Ctrl]-[Z]) to toggle between the image state before the application of the filter and after.

- ◆ You do not have to apply a filter to the entire image. Select part of an image and apply a filter to just the selected area. You can create some great looks by applying different filters to different image areas.

Creating Edge Effects

Edge effects can create some of the most interesting special effects for your images. There are two different edge effect filters, Find Edges and Glowing Edges, which create different variations of the same basic effect. Find Edges creates a primarily white image with brightly colored lines along the border between contrasting colors (the edges). Glowing Edges is just the opposite, creating a predominantly black image with brightly colored lines along the edges. The Glowing Edges effect is reminiscent of black light artwork.

To apply the Find Edges filter:

◆ From the Effects menu, choose the Stylize sub-menu and the Find Edges command.

The Find Edges filter is immediately applied to your image (**Figure 13.1**).

To apply the Glowing Edges filter:

1. From the Effects menu, choose the Stylize sub-menu and the Glowing Edges command.

2. In the Glowing Edges dialog box (**Figure 13.2**), experiment with the Edge Width, Edge Brightness, and Smoothness sliders until you are happy with the effect, as shown in the image preview.

3. Click the OK button to apply the effect to your image (**Figure 13.3**).

Figure 13.1 The original image (top), and the image with the Find Edges filter applied, which creates a sort of crayon outline effect (bottom).

Figure 13.2 The Glowing Edges dialog box.

Figure 13.3 Almost the opposite of Find Edges, the Glowing Edges filter creates this "black light" artwork.

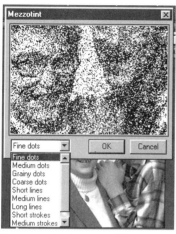

Figure 13.4 The Mezzotint dialog box.

Figure 13.5 Before (top) and after (bottom)—The Mezzotint filter converts an image to a pattern of dots, lines, or strokes.

Creating Patterns in Images

Many filter effects are based on contrast or "texture" in an image. One way to add texture to an image is to convert the image to a pattern of some sort. Two filters are great for creating patterns—the Mezzotint filter and the Mosaic filter. The Mezzotint filter is the more versatile of the two, creating patterns of dots, lines, or strokes from an image, while the Mosaic filter creates a blocky version of an image.

To convert an image to a line or dot pattern:

1. From the Effects menu, choose the Pixelate sub-menu and the Mezzotint command.

2. In the Mezzotint dialog box (**Figure 13.4**), select the type of mezzotint you want from the drop-down menu in the lower-left corner.

   Your choices are fine, medium, grainy, and coarse dots; and short, medium, and long lines or strokes.

3. Click the OK button to convert your image (**Figure 13.5**).

To use the mosaic filter:

1. From the Effects menu, choose the Pixelate sub-menu and the Mosaic command.

2. In the Mosaic dialog box (**Figure 13.6**), adjust the Cell Size as desired by dragging the slider or entering a number in the Cell Size field.

3. Click the OK button to apply the filter to your image (**Figure 13.7**).

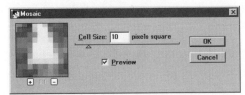

Figure 13.6 The Mosaic dialog box.

Figure 13.7 If you want a blocky version of any image, the Mosaic filter is the tool to choose.

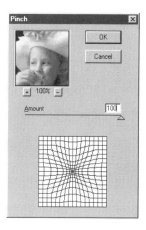

Figure 13.8 The Pinch dialog box is your digital fun house mirror factory.

Figure 13.9 The center of the image is pinched inward, or shrunk, by the Pinch filter.

Figure 13.10 Our apologies to this young lady wherever she may be. She really was lovely before we got hold of her.

Creating Distortion Effects

Of all the special effect filters, the distortion filters are probably the least useful but the most fun. With distortion filters such as Pinch, you can shrink or stretch an image or a portion of an image to create "fun house mirror" effects. The Funnel filter even lets you wrap an image around a central point, creating the illusion that you have lined an imaginary funnel with the image.

To pinch an image:

1. From the Effects menu, choose the distort sub-menu and the Pinch command.

2. In the Pinch dialog box (**Figure 13.8**), drag the slider or enter a number in the Amount field to increase or decrease the amount of pinching. (A negative pinch amount creates a "bubble" effect, similar to the Sphere filter.)

   The Pinch filter does not have a live preview checkbox as do some other filters. Instead click the + and – buttons under the dialog box preview to zoom in and out so that you can see the effect different pinch amounts will have on your image.

3. Click the OK button to apply the effect to your image (**Figure 13.9**).

✔ Tip

■ The humorous aspects of the Pinch filter can be improved by remembering that you can create selections and pinch several different areas in the same image. For example, when altering someone's face you could select and expand both eyes individually (and to varying degrees), and then select and shrink just the mouth or nose, leaving the rest of the face intact (**Figure 13.10**).

To funnel an image:

1. From the Effects menu, choose the Distort sub-menu and the Funnel command.

2. In the Funnel dialog box (**Figure 13.11**), click the – button to zoom out from the preview and see what the effect will look like.

3. Select either of the Options to create different funnel effects.

   Rectangular to Polar is the default choice and creates the type of funnel effect that you would expect, that of a rectangular image wrapped inside a funnel-shaped object.

   Polar to Rectangular creates the opposite effect, that of an image wrapped onto the outside of a funnel-shaped object (with the point of the funnel toward us).

4. Click the OK button to apply either the Rectangular to Polar (**Figure 13.12**) or the Polar to Rectangular (**Figure 13.13**) funnel effect to your image.

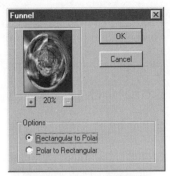

Figure 13.11 Using the dialog box preview is the best way to make sense of the Funnel filter.

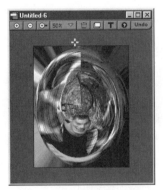

Figure 13.12 An example of an image of a man swimming, wrapped inside a funnel with the Rectangular to Polar option.

Figure 13.13 The same image wrapped outside a funnel with the Polar to Rectangular option.

CREATING DISTORTION EFFECTS

Figure 13.14 The Crystallize dialog box.

Figure 13.15 Crystallizing an image breaks the image down into large color crystals.

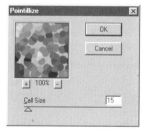

Figure 13.16 The Pointillize dialog box.

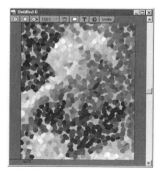

Figure 13.17 Pointillizing an image creates a more biological-looking collection of color cells—Petri dish art, as it were.

Breaking Up an Image

Another interesting effect that you can add to your image is to break the image up into clumps of color. (We know that "clumps" is an odd way to refer to color, but after working with these filters you'll see what we mean.) Both the Crystallize and Pointillize filters will break up your image into color "cells." The difference between the two is that Crystallize leaves no gaps between cells, creating a sort of, well, crystallized effect, while Pointillize leaves visible gaps and has a rounded shape to the cells, making it look more like something you'd see under a microscope. Both filters are quick and easy to use, proving that, contrary to the popular notion, breaking up is *not* hard to do.

To crystallize an image:

1. From the Effects menu, choose the Pixelate sub-menu and the Crystallize command.

2. In the Crystallize dialog box (**Figure 13.14**), drag the Cell Size slider or enter a number directly in the Cell Size field to adjust the size of the individual cells (or clumps) of color.

3. Click the OK button to apply the effect to your image (**Figure 13.15**).

To pointillize an image:

1. From the Effects menu., choose the Pixelate sub-menu and the Pointillize command.

2. In the Pointillize dialog box (**Figure 13.16**), drag the Cell Size slider or enter a number directly in the Cell Size field to adjust the size of the color cells.

3. Click the OK button to apply the effect to your image (**Figure 13.17**).

BREAKING UP AN IMAGE

Rippling Images

Subtle ripple effects can be added to your images to enhance existing backgrounds, such as water or snow, or highly exaggerated ripples can be added to create comical effects when applied to people or structures. Ripples can also be used to add a little texture to an image before applying another filter, or to create variations on standard texture effects.

Figure 13.18 The Ripple dialog box.

To add a ripple effect:

1. From the Effects menu, choose the Distort sub-menu and the Ripple command.

2. In the Ripple dialog box (**Figure 13.18**), drag the Amount slider or enter a number in the Amount field to change the amount of rippling that is applied to your image.

3. From the Size drop-down menu, select how big you want the ripples to be (small, medium, or large).

4. Click the OK button to apply the Ripple filter to your image (**Figure 13.19**).

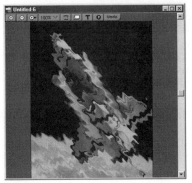

Figure 13.19 The Ripple filter has been applied to this space shuttle, creating an image Salvador Dali could be proud of.

To add a pond ripple effect:

1. From the Effects menu, choose the Distort sub-menu and the Pond Ripple command.

2. In the Pond Ripple dialog box (**Figure 13.20**), drag the Amount slider or enter a value in the Amount field to adjust the amount of rippling applied to the image.

3. Drag the Ridges slider or enter a value in the Ridges field to change the number of ripples emanating outward from the central point in your image or selected area.

    When adjusting Amount and Ridges, you will see both an image preview in the preview portion of the dialog box and an effect intensity preview in the pseudo-3D grid under the Amount and Ridges sliders.

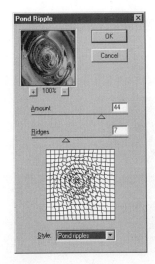

Figure 13.20 The Pond Ripple dialog box offers more choices than a simple ripple effect.

Figure 13.21 The Pond Ripple effect has added a liquid look to this space shuttle photo.

4. From the Style drop-down list, choose the type of ripples you want applied to your image.

   Around Center creates ripples that rotate around a central point, rather than moving outward from a central point.

   Out from Center creates perfectly smooth, round ripples moving out from a central point.

   Pond Ripples is the default option and creates the traditional rippling effect that you would expect, that of dropping a pebble in a still body of water, with ripples moving back toward the center as well.

5. Click the OK button to apply the Pond Ripple effect to your image (**Figure 13.21**).

Shearing Images

In traditional graphics programs, the term "shearing" usually refers to simply leaning or slanting an image in one direction or another. PhotoDeluxe adds a twist (or a curve, actually) to this concept by allowing you to slant your image in multiple directions. The Shear dialog box looks a little unusual at first, but it is actually very easy and intuitive to work with, as you will see.

To shear an image:

1. From the Effects menu, choose the Distort sub-menu and the Shear command.

   The Shear dialog box appears (**Figure 13.22**). This dialog box has three parts to it. The preview on the right side requires no explanation, and the Undefined Areas options (Wrap Around and Repeat Edge Pixels) will be immediately apparent as soon as you start shearing your images. The only thing that might not be obvious is the grid on the left side of the dialog box. The line represents the vertical "spine" of your image, and the two handles (at the top and bottom) can be moved to slant your image in one direction or another.

2. In the Shear dialog box, drag either the top or bottom "spine" handle to slant your image as desired.

3. If you do not want your image to wrap around from one side to the other (the default setting), select the Repeat Edge Pixels option under Undefined Areas, in the upper-left corner of the dialog box.

4. Click the OK button to apply the Shear filter to your image (**Figure 13.23**).

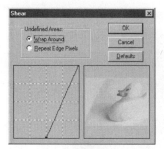

Figure 13.22 The Shear dialog box.

Figure 13.23 A simple shear effect merely slants the image.

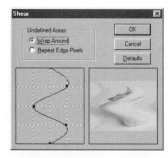

Figure 13.24 Custom shear effects can create curves or custom ripples in an image.

✔ Tip

- You can add handles to the vertical spine in the Shear dialog box by simply clicking on the spine. You can move these handles to create a curved spine, allowing you to create a wide variety of looks for your image (**Figure 13.24**). You can remove unwanted handles by dragging them out of the grid.

SHEARING IMAGES

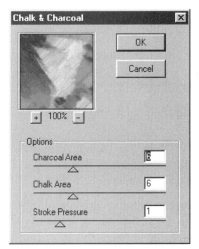

Figure 13.25 The Chalk & Charcoal dialog box.

Creating Artistic Effects

Some of the most satisfying special effect filters are those that produce an artistic effect from a scanned image. By artistic effect, we mean an effect that duplicates one created by someone with actual artistic ability (as opposed to us). Two of the filters that produce great artistic effects are Chalk & Charcoal and Colored Pencil. Both filters operate in a similar manner, but produce slightly different results.

The Chalk & Charcoal filter redraws the image using coarse lines on a gray background. You can select the chalk (background) and charcoal (foreground) colors.

The Colored Pencil filter also redraws the image on a solid (background) color of your choice. Most edges in the image are retained, but given a rough crosshatch appearance, with smoother areas of the image disappearing to reveal the background color.

To apply the Chalk & Charcoal filter:

1. Before applying this filter, select the foreground (charcoal) and background (chalk) colors that you want to use.

   Select foreground and background colors by choosing the Choose Colors command in the Effects menu, as discussed in Chapter 12, *Painting*.

2. From the Effects menus, select the Sketch sub-menu and the Chalk & Charcoal command.

3. In the Chalk & Charcoal dialog box (**Figure 13.25**), adjust the Charcoal Area, Chalk Area, and Stroke Pressure settings as desired.

   Charcoal Area determines how much of the image is filled with the foreground color.

(continues on next page)

Chalk Area determines how much of the image is filled with the background color.

Stroke Pressure determines the width and fill percentage of the strokes that are used to create the Chalk & Charcoal effect. A higher value makes the strokes more solid, revealing less of the gray background or any other strokes that might overlap.

4. Once you are happy with the settings, click the OK button to apply the Chalk & Charcoal filter to your image (**Figure 13.26**).

To apply the Colored Pencil filter:

1. From the Effects menu, choose the Artistic sub-menu and the Colored Pencil command.

2. In the Colored Pencil dialog box (**Figure 13.27**), adjust the Pencil Width, Stroke Pressure, and Paper Brightness, as desired, by dragging the sliders or entering values in the appropriate fields.

   Pencil Width determines the width of the crosshatch strokes used to create the effect.

   Stroke Pressure determines the width and fill percentage of the strokes that are used to create the effect. A higher value reveals less of the background.

   Paper Brightness changes the brightness value of the background from black (0) to white (50).

3. Click the OK button to apply the Colored Pencil filter to your image (**Figure 13.28**).

Figure 13.26 This elegantly simple effect was created with the default Chalk & Charcoal settings.

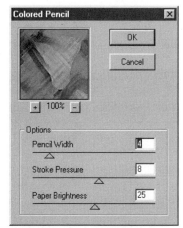

Figure 13.27 The Colored Pencil dialog box.

Figure 13.28 Another very nice effect, this time created with the default Colored Pencil settings.

CREATING ARTISTIC EFFECTS

Figure 13.29 The Accented Edges dialog box.

Creating Hand-Drawn Effects

Just as you can use artistic effects to create genuinely attractive and useful artwork from scanned images, you can use the Accented Edges and Sponge filters to create the illusion of a hand-drawn (or hand-painted, if you want to be technical about it) image.

The Accented Edges filter, as you might expect, works with the color borders (the edges) within your image and allows you to widen those edges for a hand-drawn look and also change the brightness of the edges to make it appear that they were drawn with chalk, ink, or something in between.

The Sponge filter creates an image with highly textured areas of contrasting color, creating the illusion that the image has been painted (or at least retouched) with a sponge.

To apply the Accented Edges filter:

1. From the Effects menu, choose the Brush Strokes sub-menu and the Accented Edges command (which is the only command in that sub-menu).

2. In the Accented Edges dialog box (**Figure 13.29**), adjust the Edge Width, Edge Brightness, and Smoothness as desired.

   Edge Width sets the width of the edge accents. Higher numbers create wider edges.

   Edge Brightness sets the brightness of the accent, from white (0) to black (50).

   Smoothness sets the sensitivity to the edges in the image (how closely the actual edges are followed). Smaller numbers show more edges and greater detail, while larger numbers create smoother lines.

(continues on next page)

CREATING HAND-DRAWN EFFECTS

3. Once you are happy with the results (as displayed in the preview window in the dialog box) click the OK button to apply the Accented Edges filter to your image (**Figure 13.30**).

To apply the Sponge filter:

1. From the Effects menu, choose the Artistic sub-menu and the Sponge command.

2. In the Sponge dialog box (**Figure 13.31**), adjust the Brush Size, Definition, and Smoothness as desired.

Brush Size sets the size of the holes in the sponge. Smaller numbers produce more detail in the image.

Definition controls the degree to which colors blend into each other. Lower values create more blending, while higher values create very sharp color edges.

Smoothness controls how much the image is blurred by the sponge effect. Higher values create more blurring.

3. Click the OK button to apply the Sponge filter to your image (**Figure 13.32**).

Figure 13.30 Because the Accented Edges filter makes color edges more prominent, it creates the illusion that the image was actually hand-drawn, and then colored.

Figure 13.31 The Sponge dialog box.

Figure 13.32 The Sponge filter creates a mottled and slightly blurred appearance.

CORRECTING IMAGE PROBLEMS

14

While it is true that PhotoDeluxe excels at creating special effects as shown in the previous chapter, PhotoDeluxe is also terrific when it comes to the nuts-and-bolts work of correcting image problems, such as compensating for bad lighting or poor film quality, removing red eye, repairing scratches, or sharpening blurred images.

In Chapter 4, *Modifying Images*, you learned how to follow guided activities to perform some of these tasks using a pre-set step-by-step approach. In this chapter, you will perform many of the same tasks, but you will use the advanced menus and tools.

Applying Instant Fixes

PhotoDeluxe comes with some great tools for quickly (or instantly) fixing image problems. These instant fixes are created using plug-in filters provided by Extensis, a company known for creating useful and nifty graphics software and software plug-ins. In addition to an all-in-one instant fix filter that corrects several different aspects of your image, you can also apply instant fixes to just one aspect of your image, such as brightness or sharpness.

To apply instant fixes to images:

1. Examine your image to determine if it can benefit from an instant fix.

   Images that are improved the most by the Instant Fix command are those that are too dark, too blurry, or have unwanted color casts to them (**Figure 14.1**).

2. From the Quality menu, choose Instant Fix (**Figure 14.2**).

   The image is instantly fixed, usually to an acceptable level (**Figure 14.3**). To compare the before and after versions of the image, click the Undo button in the image window toolbar.

Figure 14.1 This image could use a bit of work. It is too light and a little out of focus.

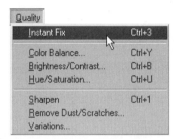

Figure 14.2 The Instant Fix command is a one-shot solution to many image problems.

Figure 14.3 After applying the Instant Fix command, this image is much more presentable.

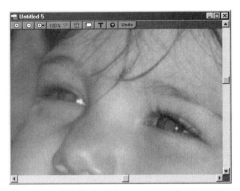

Figure 14.4 This little girl's eyes are a glowing, unnatural, and unnerving red color.

Figure 14.5 Use the Color Wand to quickly select a block of color, such as the red in her eyes.

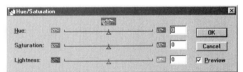

Figure 14.6 The Hue/Saturation dialog box lets you turn glowing red into subdued black.

Fixing Red Eye and Changing Eye Color

Red eye reduction is one of the most common uses for PhotoDeluxe and is often the main reason for purchasing or learning the software. Quite often, red eye is the only thing marring an otherwise perfect picture. By eliminating the red eye problem, you can rescue many otherwise unacceptable images.

In addition to simply removing unwanted red eye, you can also use this technique to change the color of your subject's eyes. This can be done subtly to create realistic changes in eye color, or more dramatically to create bizarre or supernatural effects.

To fix red eye or change eye color:

1. Use the Zoom tool (the magnifying glass) in the image window toolbar to zoom in to just the eyes in the image (**Figure 14.4**).

2. Choose Color Wand from the Selection Tools sub-menu of the Select menu, or from the drop-down list in the Selections palette.

3. Click the red area of one eye to select it.

4. If necessary, click the Add button in the Selections palette (**Figure 14.5**) and click additional areas of red to add them to the selection.

5. Once you have the red selected, choose Hue/Saturation from the Quality menu.

6. In the Hue/Saturation dialog box (**Figure 14.6**), drag the Hue slider left or right until the red color (the hue) changes to more closely match the subject's natural eye color.

(continues on next page)

7. Once the color is matched, drag the Lightness slider to the left to darken the selection almost to black.

Depending on the severity of the original red eye effect, this technique should give you an acceptable solution. For very severe red eye, there may not be enough of the actual pupil and iris showing through to be completely realistic, even with this fix.

To change eye color or create unnatural effects, simply choose different hue and lightness values in the dialog box.

8. Click OK to apply the changes to your image.

✔ Tip

■ The Color Wand selection tool is, unfortunately, not always precise enough for the intricate selections you need here. We recommend starting with the Color Wand, but then switching to the Trace selection tool, clicking the Add button in the Selections palette, and then manually tracing over any small areas of red that the Color Wand may have missed. For information on using this tool, see Chapter 9, *Selection Techniques*.

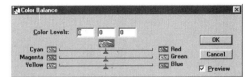

Figure 14.7 The Color Balance dialog box is an easy way to tweak the color of your image.

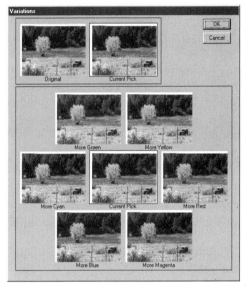

Figure 14.8 If you'd rather not see or deal with color values, the Variations dialog box lets you pick the colors that look good to you.

Adjusting Image Color

Whether caused by inadequate lighting, poor-quality film, or a bad scan, images can assume a color cast that ranges from barely noticeable to overwhelming. Fortunately, it is easy to eliminate color casts or perform other types of color correction and manipulation using the Color Balance command in the Quality menu.

To adjust image color:

1. From the Quality menu, choose Color Balance.

   The Color Balance dialog box appears (**Figure 14.7**).

2. Make sure that the Preview checkbox is selected (it is by default), and drag the Cyan/Red, Magenta/Green, or Yellow/Blue sliders to adjust the color balance in your image.

3. Once you are happy with the color, click OK to apply the changes to your image.

✔ Tip

■ In addition to manually adjusting the color balance in your image, you can use a more exploratory approach, by choosing Variations from the Quality menu. This brings up the Variations dialog box (**Figure 14.8**). In this dialog box, you click to select a variation and are then presented with variations of the variation you picked. You continue this process until you find a variation that contains the color hues you arc happiest with.

ADJUSTING IMAGE COLOR

Adjusting Brightness and Contrast

As with image color, image brightness and contrast can be adjusted easily to correct image problems caused by bad lighting, bad film, or bad scanning. Adjusting the brightness of an image increases or decreases the brightness values of all the colors in the image or selected image area, making dark blues into light blues, or blacks into grays. Adjusting the contrast of an image increases the differences between lighter and darker colors (that is, light colors get lighter and dark colors get darker).

To adjust the brightness or contrast of an image:

1. From the Quality menu, choose Brightness/Contrast.

   The Brightness/Contrast dialog box appears (**Figure 14.9**).

2. Make sure that the Preview checkbox is selected (it is by default) and drag the Brightness slider to adjust the brightness of your image.

3. Drag the Contrast slider to adjust the contrast of your image.

4. Once you are happy with your image's new brightness and contrast settings, click OK to apply the changes (**Figures 14.10** and **14.11**).

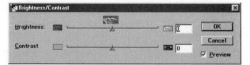

Figure 14.9 The Brightness/Contrast dialog box.

Figure 14.10 This image is dark and murky, which is great for the fish, but not so good for us.

Figure 14.11 By increasing both the brightness and contrast, this image becomes clearer and shows more detail.

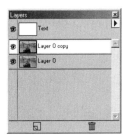

Figure 14.12 Always work on a duplicate of your image when adjusting sharpness.

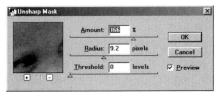

Figure 14.13 The Unsharp Mask dialog box.

Figure 14.14 Before applying the Unsharp Mask filter, this image is too blurry.

Figure 14.15 Unsharp Mask accentuates the edges in an image, making details more pronounced.

Sharpening Images

Sharpening and softening (or blurring) are two sides of the same image-correction coin. Sharpening an image makes details clearer and more distinct, and is mainly used to fix images that are blurry. Softening an image makes details fuzzy and indistinct, and is used to create artistic effects, such as blurring a background or the area around the edges of an image. Softening an image is covered in Chapter 13, *Special Effects and Filters*.

To sharpen a blurry image:

1. If the Layers palette is not visible, choose Show Layers from the View menu.

2. In the Layers palette, drag the image layer onto the New Layer icon. This creates a copy of the image layer (**Figure 14.12**). Because sharpening and softening images usually require some trial-and-error experimentation, you should never work on the original image layer.

3. Choose Unsharp Mask from the Sharpen sub-menu of the Effects menu.

4. In the Unsharp Mask dialog box that appears (**Figure 14.13**), adjust the Amount, Radius, and Threshold sliders to create a sharper version of your image.

   Amount determines how much the contrast is increased at the color edges in the image.

   Radius determines how far from the color edges the effect will be applied. For high-resolution images, a radius of 1 to 2 is recommended.

   Threshold determines how different the brightness values between pixels must be for them to be affected. Low threshold values are recommended for flesh tones and other subtle gradations of color.

5. Click OK to apply the changes to your image (**Figures 14.14** and **14.15**).

Removing Dust and Scratches

Removing dust from an image and repairing scratches are subtle tasks that enhance the overall appearance of an image. Individual changes may not be noticeable, unless a scratch is very large, but once you step back and compare the before and after versions, all of the little changes add up to a much clearer, cleaner, and more professional-looking image.

Dust and scratches can be removed in one of two ways: Using the Remove Dust/Scratches command in the Quality menu or manually retouching the affected areas. Both methods are discussed here, but for maximum image quality, we recommend manually retouching your images.

To remove dust or scratches from an image automatically:

1. If the Layers palette is not visible, choose Show Layers from the View menu.

2. In the Layers palette, drag the image layer onto the New Layer icon.

   We highly recommend working on a duplicate layer, rather than the original image. Once the work is completed to your satisfaction, you can hide or delete the original image layer.

3. Zoom to just the area that contains the dust or scratch (**Figure 14.16**).

   Using any of the selection tools, select the area around the dust or scratch that you want to repair.

   Dust and scratches are removed by blending adjacent image pixels, so some image quality is lost in the clean-up process. Therefore, it is best to select just the area that has the dust or scratch in it. The Trace selection tool is ideal for this purpose (**Figure 14.17**).

Figure 14.16 Zoom in on scratches and dust particles as much as possible to make your work easier.

Figure 14.17 The Trace selection tool lets you make changes to just the area around the scratch.

Figure 14.18 The Dust & Scratches dialog box.

Figure 14.19
The scratch has been removed, but we have lost the detail in the trees around the scratch, which is not acceptable.

Figure 14.20 Cloning begins by selecting a sampling point.

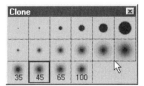

Figure 14.21 The Clone palette lets you select different brush sizes.

Figure 14.22 After cloning out the scratch using several different sampling points, we have a much better image with no loss of detail in the trees.

4. From the Quality menu, choose the Remove Dust/Scratches command.

5. In the Dust & Scratches dialog box (**Figure 14.18**), drag the Radius and Threshold sliders until the scratches or dust is no longer visible.

To avoid obvious changes to the selected area, use the lowest possible settings that will successfully remove the dust or scratches.

6. Click the OK button to apply the changes to your image (**Figure 14.19**).

To remove dust or scratches from an image manually:

1. Zoom in to the unwanted element.

2. From the Tools menu, choose Clone.

3. Drag the sampling point to an area that looks the way you want the damaged portion of your image to look (**Figure 14.20**).

4. Select a brush size in the Clone palette (**Figure 14.21**).

5. Drag over the unwanted portion of your image to replace it based on the image under the sampling point (**Figure 14.22**).

When cloning like this, it is a good idea to use several different sampling points. This prevents the obvious repetition of another image area. Also remember that you can pick different brush sizes for more detailed work.

Fixing Images using Multiple Effects

While many images have only a single problem to fix, such as removing red eye or increasing the brightness, there are always those images that require extensive work. You can fix an image using multiple effects by incorporating selections and layers into the workflow. By applying fixes to only selected areas of your image, you can (for example) brighten the dark areas of an image, fix the color in another area, remove the red eye from a third, and repair a scratch in a fourth.

Because of the hundreds of variations possible when using multiple effects on an image, the following points are not specific steps, but rather guidelines and suggestions.

To combine effects to fix a problem image:

1. Duplicate the original image layer.

2. Name the new layer "Working Image" or something like that.

3. Apply color corrections and sharpening to the entire duplicated layer.

4. Create a duplicate of this corrected layer.

5. Name this new layer "Color Correct Image" or something similar.

6. Select one area of the corrected layer.

7. Apply a filter or manual fix to just the selected area.

8. Select another area of the corrected layer.

9. Apply another filter or manual fix to the selected area.

10. Repeat as necessary.

PART 5

BUSINESS EDITION

Business Edition

While the focus of this book is on PhotoDeluxe Home Edition, we haven't forgotten all the users of the Business Edition. The two versions of PhotoDeluxe are very similar in both features and workflow, so most of the material covered in the book will apply to PhotoDeluxe Business Edition as well as to the Home Edition. This next section contains two special chapters for Business Edition users. These chapters discuss the differences in the Business Edition interface, some of the basic functionality of the Business Edition, and how to use some of the business projects that do not appear in the Home Edition.

Remember that while the two versions may look different, they perform the same basic functions and have very similar features. If you are a Business Edition user and cannot find help in these two chapters, use the index or table of contents to look for the same feature or task in the other sections of the book, and the discussion you find should serve as a guide to using the Business Edition version of the feature.

BUSINESS EDITION BASICS

This chapter and the next (Chapter 16, *Business Projects*) discuss the Business Edition of Adobe PhotoDeluxe. In particular, these chapters focus on the differences between the Home and Business versions of PhotoDeluxe. If you use the Business Edition, read through these chapters for an overview of your software, and important differences to be aware of. In general, however, the more detailed discussions of specific topics such as scanning, applying special effect filters, correcting problem images, sending images with e-mail, and so on in the first fourteen chapters in this book will also apply to your Business Edition version of PhotoDeluxe.

Installing PhotoDeluxe Business Edition

Before using PhotoDeluxe Business Edition you will first have to install the software. Installation is a simple process, and if you have ever installed any other Windows software you will have no trouble with the PhotoDeluxe Business Edition installation.

To install PhotoDeluxe Business Edition:

1. Insert the PhotoDeluxe Business Edition CD into your computer.

   Your computer will auto-load a short animation and then begin the installation process.

2. Select your desired language from the list and click the Next button.

3. At the Software License Agreement screen, click the Accept button.

   This takes you to the main installation screen (**Figure 15.1**).

4. Click the Step 1: Install PhotoDeluxe Business Edition button to start the installation process.

5. Click the Install PhotoDeluxe Business Edition button.

6. At the Welcome dialog box, click the Next button.

7. At the Setup Type dialog box (**Figure 15.2**), click the Next button.

   The default type is set to Typical, which will most likely be what you want. To customize the installation, you can click the Custom button and select individual components.

8. At the Select File Types dialog box (**Figure 15.3**), be sure to uncheck any file types that you do not want to open with

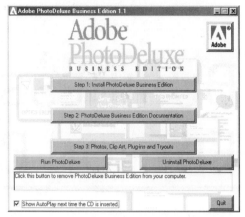

Figure 15.1 After the initial animation and language selection screen, you will be presented with this window.

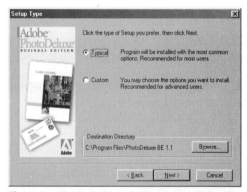

Figure 15.2 The Typical installation option will install everything you need.

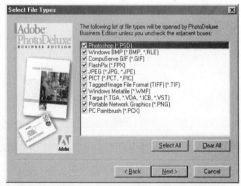

Figure 15.3 Be sure to uncheck the files types for which you do not want PhotoDeluxe Business Edition to be the default viewing application.

INSTALLING PHOTODELUXE BUSINESS EDITION

Figure 15.4 PhotoDeluxe Business Edition will recognize and work better with digital cameras if you install the Digital Camera Direct Access software.

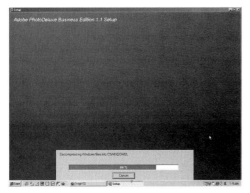

Figure 15.5 The progress bar shows how close you are to being done with the installation process.

Figure 15.6 PhotoDeluxe Business Edition also includes Adobe Type Manager.

PhotoDeluxe Business Edition, and click the Next button.

9. If you have a digital camera, click the Yes button at the next dialog box (**Figure 15.4**) to install the Digital Camera Direct Access software.

10. Enter your title, name, company, and serial number in the User Information dialog box and click the Next button.

11. Click the Yes button at the confirmation dialog box.

12. Click the Next button at the Start Copying Files dialog box.

13. The PhotoDeluxe Business Edition software will be installed to your hard drive (**Figure 15.5**).

14. At the ATM Installer dialog box (**Figure 15.6**), click the Install button to install Adobe Type Manager.

15. After ATM is installed, click the Finish button to register your software (if desired) and complete the setup process.

✔ Tip

- If you have some other graphics software, such as Adobe Photoshop, be sure to uncheck the boxes in the Select File types dialog box or *all* of your graphics files will open with PhotoDeluxe Business Edition instead of Photoshop (or whatever software you normally use), which can be very annoying. If you have already installed PhotoDeluxe Business Edition, simply re-install the software and deselect the boxes. The new settings will override the old settings.

INSTALLING PHOTODELUXE BUSINESS EDITION

The Business Edition Interface

While the basic functionality of PhotoDeluxe Business Edition is similar to that of the Home Edition, the interface is a bit different. As befits a business-oriented program, the interface is simpler and less colorful (**Figure 15.7**).

Along the left side of the interface you'll find a set of six buttons, Get & Fix Photo, Special Effects, Projects, Internet, Send & Save, and Advanced (**Figure 15.8**). The first five of these buttons display different activity bars, and the Advanced button activates the advanced menus (just as in the Home Edition).

Each activity bar (**Figure 15.9**) consists of several tabs for different types of guided activities, and each tab, once displayed, contains buttons that initiate specific guided activities. Once a guided activity has begun, the activity bar changes to display examples and instructions for each step in the guided activity (**Figure 15.10**).

Figure 15.7 The PhotoDeluxe Business Edition interface.

Figure 15.8 The buttons along the left side of the screen activate the different activity bars.

Figure 15.9 Except for some cosmetic differences, the activity bar in the Business Edition works the same as in the Home Edition.

Figure 15.10 Business Edition guided activities use the same tabbed, step-by-step approach as the Home Edition.

Figure 15.11 The image window contains a useful toolbar across the top.

As with the Home Edition, the image window (**Figure 15.11**) contains a toolbar along the top of the window. The buttons or menus in this toolbar let you change the magnification of the image, delete a selected area, change the stacking order of image elements, add text, access the online help feature, or undo the last change you made to the image.

THE BUSINESS EDITION INTERFACE

Getting Images into PhotoDeluxe Business Edition

Before you can do anything to an image in PhotoDeluxe Business Edition, you must first get the image *into* PhotoDeluxe. There are many ways to do this, from simply opening a file from disk to working through a multi-step guided activity to retrieve an image from a digital camera or scanner.

All of the techniques used to get an image into PhotoDeluxe can be found in the Get Photo tab of the Get & Fix Photo activity bar.

To open an image in PhotoDeluxe Business Edition:

1. Click the Get & Fix Photo button along the left side of the interface.

2. Click the Get Photo tab of the Get & Fix Photo activity bar (**Figure 15.12**).

3. If the file is already on your hard drive, click the Open File button in the activity bar.

   If you need to import your file from a digital camera, scanner, or other device, click the appropriate button and follow the steps shown. For more information, see Chapter 3, *Getting Images into PhotoDeluxe*.

4. In the Open dialog box that appears (**Figure 15.13**), locate and select the file that you want to open, and then click the Open button.

   An image window appears displaying the selected file (**Figure 15.14**).

Figure 15.12 The Get Photo tab provides numerous ways to bring an image into PhotoDeluxe.

Figure 15.13 This Open dialog box has a convenient image preview at the bottom.

Figure 15.14 Once opened, the image appears in its own window within PhotoDeluxe Business Edition.

Figure 15.15 The To Disk tab lets you save or export your images.

Figure 15.16 Exporting an image lets you save it in a different file format.

Saving and Exporting Images

As with any program, PhotoDeluxe files must be periodically saved to disk as you work to ensure that you do not lose your work should your computer (or your brain, in many cases) lock up. Saving is easy in PhotoDeluxe, and can be accomplished using standard methods, such as choosing Save from the File menu, or following a guided activity. You can also follow a guided activity to save an image in a non-PhotoDeluxe format (that is, to export the file for use in another application).

To save an image:

1. Click the Send & Save button along the left side of the interface.

2. Click the To Disk tab in the activity bar (**Figure 15.15**).

3. Click the Save button in the To Disk tab of the activity bar.

4. In the Save As dialog box that appears, name the file and select a location, as in any Windows Save dialog box.

5. Click the Save button to save the file.

    You can also simply choose Save from the File menu, which works as it does in any Windows application.

To export an image:

1. Click the Send & Save button along the left side of the interface.

2. Click the To Disk tab in the activity bar.

3. Click the Export button in the To Disk tab of the activity bar.

4. This starts the Export guided activity (**Figure 15.16**).

(continues on next page)

5. Click the Export tab in the activity bar.

6. Click the button that corresponds to the file format you want to use (**Figure 15.17**).

Figure 15.17 PhotoDeluxe Business Edition supports a wide variety of file formats.

7. In the resulting Save As dialog box (**Figure 15.18**), enter a name for the file. For easier access to this image, use the Add to Gallery pop-up list to select a PhotoDeluxe Gallery into which you can place a thumbnail of the image. If you do not want to add this image to a gallery, uncheck the "Add to Gallery" checkbox.

8. Click the Save button to save the file and exit the dialog box.

✔ Tip

■ To help you organize your images, you can create as many galleries as you want. Simply click the New Gallery button in the Save As dialog box, enter a name for your new gallery in the Create Gallery dialog box (**Figure 15.19**), and click the Create Gallery button. Make as many new galleries as you want, and then click the Done button to return to the Save As dialog box. These new galleries will appear in the "Add to Gallery" pop-up list.

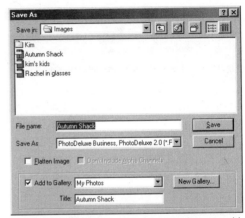

Figure 15.18 The Save As dialog box also lets you add images to galleries.

Figure 15.19 Creating new image galleries is easy, as shown in this simple dialog box.

Figure 15.20 The To Printer tab lets you print your images in a variety of ways.

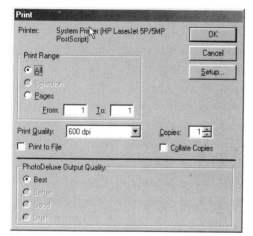

Figure 15.21 PhotoDeluxe Business Edition uses a standard Print dialog box.

Printing Images

It's easy to print images using PhotoDeluxe. Simply use the Print button in the To Printer tab of the Send & Save activity bar, or choose Print from the File menu.

To print an image:

1. Click the Send & Save button on the left side of the screen.

2. Click the To Printer tab in the activity bar (**Figure 15.20**).

3. In the standard Print dialog box that appears (**Figure 15.21**), change the Print Range, Print Quality, or any other settings that you want to change.

4. Click OK to send the image information to your printer.

PRINTING IMAGES

183

Understanding the Advanced Options

The advanced options in PhotoDeluxe Business Edition are very similar to their Home Edition counterparts. The Advanced button is a toggle that shows or hides the advanced menus. Before using any of the advanced options, you will need to click the Advanced button on the left side of the screen to display the advanced menus. Clicking this button again hides the advanced menus and any visible advanced palettes.

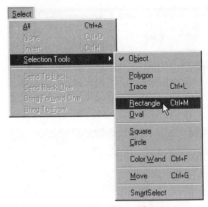

Figure 15.22 Use this advanced menu to choose your desired selection tool.

To make a selection:

1. Click the Advanced button on the left side of the screen.

2. From the Select menu, choose the Selection Tools sub-menu and the Rectangle command (or any other, depending on exactly what you want to select) (**Figure 15.22**).

3. In your image, press and drag to create a rectangular selection around the area that you want to work with (**Figure 15.23**).

   Once a selection is made, effects or commands will only affect the portion of the image within the boundaries of the selection. For a more detailed discussion of the selection tools and their uses, see Chapter 9, *Selection Techniques*.

Figure 15.23 Press and drag to create a rectangular "frame" around the part of the image you want to work with.

To add a layer:

1. If the advanced menus are not visible, click the Advanced button on the left side of the screen.

2. From the View menu, choose Show Layers.

3. The Layers palette appears (**Figure 15.24**).

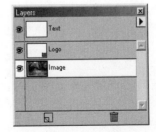

Figure 15.24 The Layers palette lists all layers in the image.

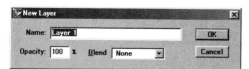

Figure 15.25 When creating a new layer, be sure to give it a more meaningful name than just "Layer 1."

Figure 15.26 The Effects menu has dozens of different categories and filters that you can apply to your image.

Figure 15.27 Two seconds after applying the Chalk & Charcoal filter this image looks like it was drawn by hand.

4. Click the New Layer button at the bottom of the palette.

This button looks like a piece of paper with one corner folded over.

5. In the New Layer dialog box (**Figure 15.25**), name the layer and click OK.

For a discussion of the Opacity and Blend options in this dialog box, as well as all the things you can do with layers, see Chapter 10, *Combining Images.*

To apply a filter effect:

1. If the advanced menus are not visible, click the Advanced button on the left side of the screen.

2. From the Effects menu (**Figure 15.26**), choose a category of effects and a specific effect that you want to apply to your image or selected image area.

If the effect that you choose has options, a dialog box will appear. Otherwise, the effect is simply applied to your image (**Figure 15.27**). For a much more detailed discussion of applying special effects, see Chapter 13, *Special Effects and Filters.*

BUSINESS
PROJECTS

One of the distinguishing features of the
Business Edition of PhotoDeluxe is that all of
the guided activities are business oriented, as
you might expect. Despite the different look
of the Business Edition interface, the way you
follow guided activities is the same as following guided activities in the Home Edition
(that is, you simply click on the activity you
want to follow, click each instruction tab in
order, and follow the instructions provided
on each tab).

In this chapter you will learn how to complete
several business projects. PhotoDeluxe
Business Edition actually comes with many
more projects, but each one can be completed
using the general steps outlined here.

Creating Business Cards

PhotoDeluxe Business Edition makes it easy to design business cards that incorporate photographs or other color images. The Business Edition includes numerous business card templates, which contain placeholder text and graphic elements to frame any photographs that you wish to add to the business card.

The basic process for creating a business card involves selecting a template, adding one or more photographs, and then editing the text to reflect your own corporate information.

To create a business card:

1. Click the Projects button on the left side of the screen.

2. Click the Cards tab in the activity bar (**Figure 16.1**).

3. Click the Business Cards button to begin the Business Cards guided activity.

4. Click the Choose Business Card tab in the activity bar.

5. Click the Choose Card button.

6. In the Templates palette that appears (**Figure 16.2**), locate and double-click the business card template that you want to use.

   Double-clicking the template opens an untitled copy of the template for you to work with.

7. Once a template is open, click the Add tab in the activity bar.

8. Open the image that you want to add to the template, using any of the buttons or menus in the Add tab.

   The Open File button is discussed in Chapter 15, *Business Edition Basics*, and the other buttons and menus are discussed in Chapter 3, *Getting Images into*

Figure 16.1 Business cards are just one of many types of cards you can create.

Figure 16.2 This palette contains templates for all sorts of different business cards.

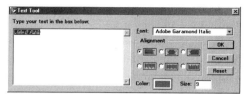

Figure 16.3 Change the text on the card template using the Text Tool dialog box.

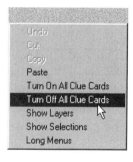

Figure 16.4 Turning off all the Clue Cards speeds up your work once you know what you are doing.

PhotoDeluxe. Once you've added the image, it can be moved, resized, and repositioned normally.

9. Double-click on any block of text in the template to open the Text Tool dialog box (**Figure 16.3**).

10. Edit the text as desired, and change the font, alignment, color, and size, if desired, then click the OK button to return to the template.

11. Repeat steps 9 and 10 to edit the remaining text placeholders on the template.

✔ Tip

■ As you work through the various projects described in this chapter, Clue Card dialog boxes will appear. While a good idea initially, these Clue Cards can get annoying after a while. To disable all of these Clue Card dialog boxes, right-click anywhere in the Business Edition interface and choose Turn Off All Clue Cards from the shortcut menu (**Figure 16.4**).

CREATING BUSINESS CARDS

Creating Letterhead or Envelopes

The process for creating letterhead or envelopes is similar to that for creating business cards. You start by selecting a template, add a photograph or other image, and then edit the text to reflect your information.

To create letterhead or an envelope:

1. Click the Projects button on the left side of the screen.

2. Click the Forms tab in the activity bar.

3. Click the Letterhead or Envelopes button to begin the guided activity.

4. Click the Choose Letterhead or Choose Envelope tab (**Figure 16.5**) in the activity bar.

5. Click the Choose Letterhead or Choose Envelope button.

6. In the Templates palette that appears (**Figure 16.6**), locate and double-click the letterhead or envelope template that you want to use.

   Double-clicking the template opens an untitled copy of the template for you to work with.

7. Once a template is open, click the Add tab in the activity bar.

8. Open the image that you want to add to the template, using any of the buttons or menus in the Add tab.

9. Resize and reposition the image as desired.

   You can move images by dragging the middle of the image, resize them by dragging the corner selection handles, or rotate them by dragging the round rotation handles (**Figure 16.7**).

Figure 16.5 Creating an envelope is a simple three-step process.

Figure 16.6 All business projects involve choosing a template from a palette like this one.

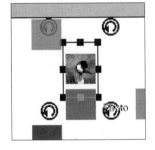

Figure 16.7 As with any image, images used in business projects can be repositioned, resized, and reshaped using these handles.

Figure 16.8 Get used to this dialog box, as you will see it in just about every business project you use.

10. Double-click on any block of text in the template to open the Text Tool dialog box (**Figure 16.8**).

11. Edit the text as desired, and change the font, alignment, color, and size, if desired, then click the OK button to return to the template.

12. Repeat steps 10 and 11 to edit the remaining text placeholders on the template.

CREATING LETTERHEAD OR ENVELOPES

Creating Web Elements

PhotoDeluxe Business Edition easily creates Web elements, such as buttons, banners, and backgrounds. However, these Web elements are very basic and contain no animation of any kind. Your banners will not animate and your buttons will have no rollover effects. (A rollover is when the button image changes when you point to it, such as changing color or looking pushed in.) If you want to create animated Web elements, we recommend using Adobe ImageReady, which is included as part of Photoshop 5.5, or Adobe ImageStyler, which is available for purchase as a stand-alone product.

To create a Web banner or button:

1. Click the Projects button on the left side of the screen.

2. Click the Web tab in the activity bar.

3. Click the Banners or Buttons button to begin the guided activity.

4. Click the Choose Banner or Choose Button tab in the activity bar.

5. Click the Choose Banner or Choose Button button (**Figure 16.9**).

6. In the Templates palette that appears, locate and double-click the banner or button template that you want to use. Double-clicking the template opens an untitled copy of the template for you to work with (**Figure 16.10**).

7. Once a template is open, click the Add tab in the activity bar.

8. Open the image that you want to add to the template, using any of the buttons or menus in the Add tab.

9. Resize and reposition the image as desired.

Figure 16.9 While PhotoDeluxe doesn't position itself as a Web graphics tool, you can create simple buttons and banners.

Figure 16.10 Here, a button template has been opened and awaits an image to make it complete.

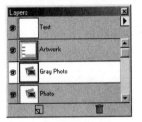

Figure 16.11 Use PhotoDeluxe layers to hold button variations which can save you a step when you use another program to create rollover effects.

✔ Tip

■ As mentioned earlier, PhotoDeluxe does not support animated Web graphics, such as animated banners or rollovers. However, many of these effects are created in other programs using layers, which PhotoDeluxe does support. If you want to create Web animations from your PhotoDeluxe images, you can give yourself a headstart by adding layers and using those layers to hold the animated states of your image (**Figure 16.11**). (By animated states, we simply mean the versions of your image that you want to use when you prepare your animation.) For example, to create a simple rollover effect, you might create a red button, and then on another layer change the button color to blue. In your Web animation program, you can simply hide the red layer and reveal the blue layer to create the illusion that the button is changing color when it is pointed to.

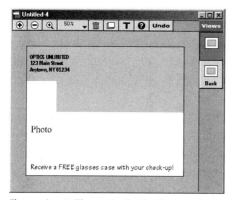

Figure 16.12 Unlike most other business projects, direct mail cards have two or more sides, so make use of the View buttons on the right side of this image window.

Creating Marketing Materials

In addition to standard printed business materials such as business cards, letterhead, and envelopes, PhotoDeluxe Business Edition can also create a wide variety of marketing materials. Some of these marketing materials include flyers, coupons, direct mail cards, and t-shirt transfers.

Flyers and coupons are created like any other business project, and so don't need to be discussed here, but direct mail cards are created a little differently, and you have a little more control over how you work with them and their final look.

To create a direct mail card:

1. Click the Projects button on the left side of the screen.

2. Click the Promote tab in the activity bar.

3. Click the Direct Mail Cards button to begin the guided activity.

4. Click the Layout tab in the activity bar.

5. Click the Postcard or Self Seal Mailer button to choose the layout you want to use.

   Unlike other business projects, you will not be presented with a palette of templates at this point. Your choice here determines which set of templates will appear in step 8.

6. Click the Style tab.

7. Click the Choose Style button.

8. In the palette that appears, locate and double-click on the postcard or self-seal mailer template that you want to use.

9. Click the View tab in the activity bar to read about the new View buttons on the right side of the image window (**Figure 16.12**).

(continues on next page)

10. Click the Add tab in the activity bar.

11. Open the image that you want to add to the template, using any of the buttons or menus in the Add tab.

12. Resize and reposition the image as desired.

13. Use the View buttons on the right side of the template to switch views (**Figure 16.13**), and repeat steps 10 and 11 until you are happy with the images on your direct mail card.

14. Double-click any text block on the template to open the Text Tool dialog box (**Figure 16.14**).

15. Edit the text as desired, and reformat as desired using the Font, Alignment, Color, and Size options.

16. Click the OK button to return to your direct mail card.

17. Repeat steps 14 through 16 for other text blocks on your direct mail card.

18. Use the View buttons to check and change the text in other views, as well.

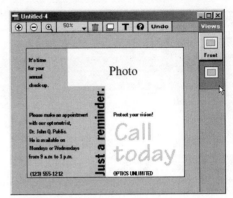

Figure 16.13 The back side of the direct mail postcard.

Figure 16.14 The omnipresent Text Tool dialog box is especially important for a direct mail card, since it will contain a lot of text.

INDEX

O

object selection tool, 98
OK button, 22
opacity, 4CP, 107, 119
Opacity check box (New Layer dialog box), 107
Open dialog box, 25, 180
Open File button, 180
opening
    images in Business Edition version, 180
    photo files, 25
output, 74
Oval selection tool, 99
overlay blend mode, 1CP

P

Page Curl filter, 3CP, 132
page icon (Layers palette), 106
Page Setup dialog box, 86
PageMill, 82–83
painting, 135–148
    cloning image areas, 43, 139–140
    colorizing black and white images, 147–148
    creating text labels, 141–142
    erasing image and effects, 138
    smudging images, 143–144
    tracing image elements, 101, 145–146
    using painting tools, 135, 136–137
Paper Brightness option (Colored Pencil dialog box), 160
paper size for printing, 88
Patchwork filter, 3CP, 122
PDF files, 8
Pencil Width option (Colored Pencil dialog box), 160
photo album pages, 54–55
photo list, 18
Photo Size dialog box, 82
photo-CDs, 14
PhotoDeluxe. *See* Adobe PhotoDeluxe
photographs
    connecting digital camera to
        PhotoDeluxe, 26
    curling corners of image, 3CP, 132

opening file on disk, 25
removing dust and scratches from, 45–46, 170–171
removing noise from, 45–46
removing red eye, 5CP, 44, 165–166
restoring and retouching, 42–43
retrieving images from My Photos album, 24
scanning into PhotoDeluxe, 27
sharing on Web, 68–69
using Get & Fix Photo button, 23, 32
using sample, 17, 28
PhotoParades, 60–62
    creating, 60–61
    playing, 62
    themes for, 61
    viewing titles and captions in Carousel mode, 62
Photoshop file format, 77
PICT file format, 77
Pinch dialog box, 3CP, 153
pixel-based graphics
    capturing with digital cameras, 15
    defined, 12
    resolution and pixels, 12–13
playing PhotoParades, 62
PNG file format, 77
Pointillize filter, 3CP, 126, 155
Polar to Rectangular option (Funnel dialog box), 154
Polygon selection tool, 100
Pond Ripple dialog box, 156
pond ripple effects, 156–157
Post to Web album window, 69
postcards
    creating, 50–51
    direct mail, 193–194
    Web-based, 66–67
previewing
    images before printing, 87
    unopened photo files, 25, 180
Print dialog box, 90, 183
Print Multiple dialog box, 90
print page, 86
Print Preview dialog box, 87

INDEX

INDEX